THE BEST CLASS You Never TAUGHT

ASCD MEMBER BOOK

Many ASCD members received this book as a
member benefit upon its initial release.

Learn more at: **www.ascd.org/memberbooks**

ALEXIS WIGGINS

THE BEST CLASS You Never TAUGHT

How SPIDER WEB DISCUSSION Can Turn Students into Learning Leaders

With a Foreword by Jay McTighe

 Alexandria, Virginia USA

1703 N. Beauregard St. • Alexandria, VA 22311-1714 USA
Phone: 800-933-2723 or 703-578-9600 • Fax: 703-575-5400
Website: www.ascd.org • E-mail: member@ascd.org
Author guidelines: www.ascd.org/write

Deborah S. Delisle, *Executive Director;* Robert D. Clouse, *Managing Director, Digital Content & Publications;* Stefani Roth, *Publisher;* Genny Ostertag, *Director, Content Acquisitions;* Julie Houtz, *Director, Book Editing & Production;* Darcie Russell, *Editor;* Khanh Pham, *Graphic Designer;* Mike Kalyan, *Director, Production Services;* Cynthia Stock, *Typesetter;* Kyle Steichen, *Senior Production Specialist*

All web links in this book are correct as of the publication date below but may have become inactive or otherwise modified since that time. If you notice a deactivated or changed link, please e-mail books@ascd.org with the words "Link Update" in the subject line. In your message, please specify the web link, the book title, and the page number on which the link appears.

PAPERBACK ISBN: 978-1-4166-2468-4   ASCD product #117017
PDF E-BOOK ISBN: 978-1-4166-2470-7; see Books in Print for other formats.
Quantity discounts are available: e-mail programteam@ascd.org or call 800-933-2723, ext. 5773, or 703-575-5773. For desk copies, go to www.ascd.org/deskcopy.

ASCD Member Book No. FY18-1 (Sep 2017 PSI+). ASCD Member Books mail to Premium (P), Select (S), and Institutional Plus (I+) members on this schedule: Jan, PSI+; Feb, P; Apr, PSI+; May, P; Jul, PSI+; Aug, P; Sep, PSI+; Nov, PSI+; Dec, P. For current details on membership, see www.ascd.org/membership.

Library of Congress Cataloging-in-Publication Data

Names: Wiggins, Alexis.
Title: The best class you never taught : how spider web discussion can turn
    students into learning leaders / Alexis Wiggins with a foreword by Jay
    McTighe.
Description: Alexandria, Virginia : ASCD, [2017] | Includes bibliographical
    references and index.
Identifiers: LCCN 2017026416 (print) | LCCN 2017036528 (ebook) | ISBN
    9781416624707 (PDF) | ISBN 9781416624684 (pbk.)
Subjects: LCSH: Group work in education. | Discussion—Study and teaching. |
    Inquiry-based learning. | Active learning. | Education—Philosophy.
Classification: LCC LB1032 (ebook) | LCC LB1032 .W53 2017 (print) | DDC
    371.3/6--dc23
LC record available at https://lccn.loc.gov/2017026416

26 25 24 23 22 21 20 19 18 17   1 2 3 4 5 6 7 8 9 10 11 12

*For my dad, who told me
to write and gave me the
confidence to teach from the heart.*

THE BEST CLASS YOU NEVER TAUGHT

Foreword by Jay McTighe..ix

Acknowledgments...xi

Introduction.. 1

1. Why We Need Spider Webbers 3

2. The First Spider Web Discussion 16

3. The First Few Weeks of Discussion 43

4. Roadblocks Early On: Shy Kids and Superstars 67

5. Roadblocks Later On: That One Tough Class 93

6. Assessment Is a Tool, Not a Weapon...111

7. Benefits of Spider Web Discussion...130

8. Looking Ahead: A Year of Spider Web Discussion 150

References...159

Index...161

About the Author..164

FOREWORD

I had the privilege of working closely with Dr. Grant Wiggins for nearly twenty years before his untimely death in 2015. Grant dedicated his professional life to making education more thoughtful, engaging, and authentic—for learners and teachers alike. Grant was a true intellectual whose ideas influenced educators around the world. With Grant's passing, our profession lost an extraordinary thought leader . . . and I lost my best friend.

Thankfully, Grant's daughter Alexis has picked up the baton and continues the Wigginses' tradition of thoughtful professional writing. In *The Best Class You Never Taught*, she describes her process of creating a classroom culture that supports shared inquiry, encourages deep thinking, invites respectful dialogue, and strengthens student autonomy. The book includes insights gained from her many years of teaching experience, professional readings, action research, reflections on practice, and numerous professional conversations. The result is a protocol and a compendium of associated tools for initiating and implementing Spider Web Discussions in the classroom.

Wiggins makes it clear that the Spider Web Discussion is much more than another pedagogical "technique." It is grounded in firm beliefs about educational outcomes and the nature of meaningful learning. Her work is a testament to the contention that modern schooling must do more than transmit information. In a world in which we can search much of the world's knowledge on a smartphone, educators must seek to develop in students the so-called 21st century skills of critical and creative thinking, collaboration, and communication. Teachers must transition from being mere transmitters of content to facilitators of conceptual understanding. Wiggins's recommended methodology reflects a constructivist conception of learning drawn from research in cognitive psychology and neuroscience, in which students must be actively engaged in personal and collective meaning making.

Through personal anecdotes, Wiggins describes her educational journey of exploring the Harkness method, formulating the Spider Web Discussion process, and working to develop the cultural and behavioral dimensions needed for its success in a classroom. She encourages readers to have the courage to embark on new methodologies and reassures them of the value of moving out of one's pedagogical comfort zone and gradually turning over the reins of learning to students.

The book is scholarly without being "ivory tower"; practical without being simplistic. Wiggins cites relevant research with the authority and assurance of an academic while offering no nonsense advice with the clarity and confidence of a veteran teacher. Simply put, *The Best Class You Never Taught* provides eminently practical and proven techniques for engaging respectful discussions, promoting meaning making and reflection, and building capacities for self-directed learning. Your students will thank you for reading this book and bringing its ideas to life in your classroom. And Alexis's dad would be so proud.

Jay McTighe
Coauthor of *Understanding by Design*

ACKNOWLEDGMENTS

First and foremost I'd like to thank Jay McTighe for his encouragement, time, and advice. This book never would have been published if it weren't for you, and I thank you deeply for all you've done to guide me, both professionally and personally.

Thank you to Genny Ostertag, an editor with her roots in the literary world, like me, who seemed to understand better than I did what the vision for this book was and pushed me to realize it. Thanks to Darcie Russell for her excellent editing skills, which greatly improved the original manuscript and taught me a thing or two about economy of words. And thank you to the rest of the team at ASCD for their many contributions to the book.

Thank you to the teachers and students who wrote testimonials about their experiences: Eric Mazur, Liam Trimm, Nellie Bridge, Ali Ani, Beth Dagitses, Kim McKnee, Rayyan Amine, and Crystal Van Cleef. Thank you to those educators who trialed the method or provided resources, anecdotes, and feedback: Bettina Meyer, Sara Bjork, Chris Watson, Adam Cross, David Lawrence, Jaison Norris, Mike Moody, Maha Al Ansari, and Janelle Schmidt. Thank you to the former and current English department members at the Masters School in Dobbs Ferry, New York, for lighting the spark for me with student discussion. Thanks to Jane Segre at the American School of Milan, Linda Menton at King's Academy (Jordan), and Scott Hayden at International Community School (Bangkok) for helping me spread the message. All of you have played a role in making this method better; I feel blessed to have a network of wonderful former students, colleagues, and thinkers like you.

Thank you to Mike Maher, Steve Popp, Gillian Crane, and the English department at The John Cooper School for giving me and my ideas a home. Thanks to all the Cooper faculty, staff, and students for making it a wonderful place to teach and learn.

A big thank you to one of my mentors, Elizabeth Rossini, for her professional and emotional support over the last five years; I am always grateful for your education insights and career advice, as well as your friendship.

An enormous thank you to Tracy Hill, who I was blessed to work alongside, learn from, and befriend. You helped me as a sounding board, a networker, and an honest feedback giver. You inspire me with how often you multiply others' talents and with your thoughtful, generous nature. I am grateful for the time and energy you have given me and my projects; your fingerprints are all over them.

I'd like to thank my grandparents, Jean Shaak, Guy Wiggins, and Dorothy Wiggins, for their unconditional love and support over the years. You have always been my biggest fans. Nana and Guy, I'm so grateful for your wisdom and vitality. If I model myself after you, I will still be writing, teaching, and presenting in my 90s.

I'd like to thank my mother, Joanna Draugsvold, for showing me that great teachers are the ones that change students' lives. I'm amazed by how many former students of yours wax poetic about your classes, even decades later.

I'd like to thank my father, Grant Wiggins, for being my educational hero. I miss your insights, encouragement, and "pain-in-the-ass educator" stance every day. You have left an indelible mark on education and all of us in the field. This book would never have been written if it weren't for you. Thanks, Dad.

I'd like to thank my two boys, Elios and Amadeo, for their love and patience throughout this long book-writing process. I'm sorry if I had to miss family time to work, but your hugs and laughter always made up for the many hours spent writing and editing.

Finally, I'd like to thank my husband, Diego, for his support and encouragement with this book and all my professional endeavors. I never doubted myself, Diego, because you never doubted me, acting as if there were no other possibility but success. Thank you for that measure of confidence and for always knowing when and how to make me laugh.

INTRODUCTION

One of my pet peeves as an educator is the lack of practical applications for all the great ideas out there in the field of education. When I go to conferences or attend an inservice day, I almost always have the same experience: I witness a lot of inspirational ideas, spirited keynote addresses, and outside-the-box thinking. I often come away from these conventions admiring the work of the presenters and speakers, having enjoyed their insights immensely, and excited about what I've learned.

But then it's Monday, and I'm back in class. Now what? How do I take the wonderful, inspirational, and funny ideas of someone like crowd-pleaser Sir Ken Robinson and translate that to the 23 students I have staring back at me in class the next week?

I call it the "Monday Morning Test." I love inspiration as much as any teacher, and I'm so glad there are presenters and consultants out there inspiring the masses. But somewhere between inspiration and practicality there seems to be a gap into which most of us educators fall—we, too, believe our children should have more creativity in their day-to-day education. But how, exactly, should we introduce that creativity? I want nothing more than to inspire learning in my classroom through technology, but how do I translate that cool presentation on technology trends at my latest PD session into something I can use Monday morning in my classroom with a clear, beneficial effect on my students?

The aim of *The Best Class You Never Taught* is just that. I want you to read this short book and have all the tools you need to start Spider Web Discussion (SWD) on Monday morning. I want you to finish this book and know exactly what this method is, how to use it, and how to share it with others if you want to. That simple. I believe in the democracy of ideas, and this book is a way of sharing one of the most effective, game-changing tools I have encountered as a classroom teacher.

Should you ever want further training in Spider Web Discussion to take your understanding of the method to a deeper level, I welcome you to join one of my workshops, but it isn't necessary. I have designed this book to be everything I look for when I'm on the prowl for great, clear, practical approaches to pedagogy: short, to the point, practical, and filled with tips for how to approach this method from the very first day.

Chapter 1 explores why this method is important and useful and explains some of the research behind it. Beginning with Chapter 2, and continuing for the rest of the book, you will find a step-by-step approach for teachers that details how to go about implementing Spider Web Discussion in the classroom. The book is structured chronologically through the experience of an educator wanting to use Spider Web Discussion: Chapter 2 introduces the method and its applications and what a teacher can expect for her first Spider Web Discussion. Chapter 3 helps a teacher navigate the first few weeks of using the method in the classroom. Chapter 4 addresses some of the typical challenges that crop up in the first few days and weeks; Chapter 5 addresses the longer-term challenges a teacher might face and proposes several suggestions for how to approach them. Chapter 6 deals exclusively with the unique assessment strategy that helps make Spider Web Discussion such a powerful tool for teaching effective collaboration. Chapter 7 highlights the many benefits, both expected and unexpected, of designing a classroom culture through the method. And the last chapter, Chapter 8, lays out what a year of Spider Web Discussion might look like from the teacher's perspective. Each chapter includes a vignette describing a typical scenario that teachers and students might face, provides details on that chapter's focus, has a section on pertinent research, offers both practical applications and advanced applications, shares a real testimonial from teachers and students who have used the method, and culminates with a section called "Big Takeaway" that summarizes the highlights of the chapter.

My hope is that, like so many educators I know, you will come away from your first Spider Web Discussion a little shocked. I never tire of teachers saying to me, surprised, "I didn't know the students could *do* that." They can. You will be amazed how much they can do in Spider Web Discussion with your guidance, the criteria, and greater autonomy.

1 WHY WE NEED SPIDER WEBBERS

Karen graduated first in her class from Yale and went on to get her MBA from Harvard Business School. She was given the chance to publish some of her research while at Harvard, which led to an offer to head a multinational bank's institute on leadership. She packed her bags and moved halfway across the world to oversee the leadership branch of the bank's corporate offices. Part of her job was to travel the region to conduct interviews and surveys with industry leaders to learn and understand the hallmarks of leadership and to determine some of the personal and professional challenges keeping talented leaders, especially women, from top leadership tracks. In addition to this work, she was tasked with recruiting and hiring the best and brightest candidates for research and development work—keeping in mind that the best candidates on paper may not have key interpersonal skills.

Karen realized quickly that applicants' résumés were not helpful in determining who would be the best hires. She had a host of candidates from topnotch business schools to choose from, but many applicants lacked the sophisticated, nuanced communication skills needed in corporate leadership. She began to look for only two things in potential hires: excellent written and oral communication skills. Karen felt that new hires could learn the business of banking on the job, but the skills of asking good questions, listening, and communicating were invaluable to her team and she did not have the resources to teach these skills. The company needed employees who had honed their communication and social skills; the rest of their résumé was just window dressing.

Consider the following four excerpts from articles in the news media between the years 2013–2015, and see if you can spot the common thread:

> *Being able to read the room is such a crucial skill, adds Phunware sales executive Mike Snavely, that he's willing to hire people who don't know much about technology if they have a gift for relating to other people.* (Anders, 2005, p. 2)

> *What we care about is . . . do you step back and stop leading, do you let someone else? Because what's critical to be an effective leader in this environment is you have to be willing to relinquish power.* (Laszlo Bock [Google] in Friedman, 2014, p. SR11)

> *You no longer have that strict hierarchical culture in the cockpit, where the captain was king and everyone blindly followed his orders. It's team oriented nowadays.* (Brennan, 2013, p. TR3)

> *Young people have not been well prepared for adult life today unless they are comfortable and well practiced in addressing collaboratively the kinds of problems and objectives that 21st century life poses.* (Kuhn, 2015, p. 51)

These articles range in focus from hiring in the technology sector to aviation safety to education research, but they all highlight one key point: today's jobs demand effective collaboration. Today's most competitive jobs go to candidates who can both lead and listen, innovate and question, see the big picture as well as the small details.

Are we doing this? Not that well. Unfortunately, we in education are prone to thinking that simply imposing a new structure or method will produce positive results. Those of us working in K–12 settings know this story well: in an effort to improve learning, many schools or districts decide to promote a new initiative, such as Socratic seminar, the Workshop Model, or an iPad for every student, and offer some initial training and follow up with a handful of meetings. But that is usually it. We seldom perform action research to test whether our initiative is effective at improving student learning. We rarely offer tiered, multifaceted, well-designed professional development to support the teaching faculty and administrators in how best to carry out the initiative over time. And, sadly, most of us have experienced the institutional cynicism that comes with the "flavor-of-the-year" initiatives that surge at the beginning of every new school year and fizzle over time. We've also experienced the deflation that happens when the leaders championing new initiatives move on without structures in place to ensure continued success.

Spider Web Discussion does not aim to be a quick fix. It isn't about introducing a new, trendy structure in your classroom. It's not meant to be a box that is simply ticked on a supervisor's observation checklist.

Spider Web Discussion is a classroom philosophy, not a one-off activity. It's a culture. It's about understanding that learning is a complex process that plays out over time, through allowing students to grapple with challenging questions, ideas, and people. The process of Spider Web Discussion trains students to work together collaboratively in solving problems and to self-assess that process. The result is deep, high-level inquiry led and assessed by the students themselves, whether they are in 2nd grade social studies or high school geometry. Teachers using Spider Web Discussion aim to create authentic collaborators, communicators, and self-evaluators through ongoing, sustained discussion and assessment.

I have been using or training other teachers to use Spider Web Discussion in classrooms for more than 10 years and I believe it is the single most powerful tool in my teaching toolbox. When I read the four excerpts (p. 4), I'm struck by how well Spider Web Discussion achieves each of the valued skills and abilities cited. In my experience, it goes further than those crucial skills; if done right, it instills a magical feeling in the classroom, one where students feel safe and excited to share their deepest intellectual questions and ideas, where students realize they are on the same team, working toward a common goal, no longer competing for airtime or top grades. This awareness produces a sense of community and an ethical space in which true inquiry becomes possible.

Think of the aviation example: flight safety is better now due to the collaborative process. All who fly benefit from the fact that the industry now values collaboration over traditional power structures—and the stakes are pretty high when you are talking about plane safety. Systems thinking has evolved; today's employees must be prepared to value each other's input, seek varied voices, consider multiple perspectives, and "relinquish power," as noted by Bock, a Google executive. We should be giving these practices top billing in our classroom—not merely as structures, but as cultures and practices that are taught, learned, and assessed on a regular basis.

Why do we need Spider Webbers? Precisely for the reasons cited in the news excerpts. We owe it to our students to train them in—not just superficially expose them to—how to collaborate successfully. This is *the* vital skill for the future.

And while Spider Web Discussion teaches complex skills like teamwork, empathy, citing evidence, and self-assessment, the method is simple. You only need a rubric, a pencil, and some paper to get started.

A Brief History of Spider Web Discussion

The Origins of Harkness Method

In my mid-20s, I found myself teaching high school English at The Masters School, in New York's Hudson Valley. The Masters School was different from the other schools I had taught in; it was a Harkness school, which is a school that uses Socratic seminar discussion in its classrooms. I was daunted by the new-to-me notion that students were meant to run their own discussions.

The history of the Harkness method can be traced to one of America's preeminent New England prep schools, Philips Exeter Academy. In 1930, a wealthy donor named Edward Harkness gave the school a generous gift with the stipulation that it be used to promote a new style of classroom instruction. He wrote: "What I have in mind is [a classroom] where [students] could sit around a table with a teacher who would talk with them and instruct them by a sort of tutorial or conference method, where [each student] would feel encouraged to speak up. This would be a real revolution in methods" ("The Harkness Gift"). What developed from this idea were oval tables around which all students and the teacher were seated equally, able to see each other's eyes, fostering discussion.

At the Masters School, the oval table tradition lived on; every classroom, even science and math classrooms, had large oval tables in the center of the room, around which students debated, discussed, and problem solved (science rooms were purpose-built with labs in the back and oval tables in the front).

But the table is not the point; schools do not need a specific table to foster discussion. The purpose of the Harkness method is to actively engage students in their learning process through the exchange of ideas and group problem solving. For the first time in my career, I was asked to shift my role from fount of knowledge to facilitator. The challenge posed to me for the first time as an educator was entirely novel to me: how could I get the students *themselves* to uncover the most pertinent, key understandings in the content we studied with as little hand-holding from me as possible?

I began by using a rubric that a colleague shared with me, which flipped much of the conventional approach to class participation on its head. The rubric required students to engage in fairly standard practices during discussion, such as listening and being respectful, referring to the text to support their point, and avoiding interrupting others. One interesting element is that it asked for (more or less) equal participation during discussion, meaning the shy kids would need to make an effort to speak up and the chatty kids would need to make an effort to allow others some space to do so. The real kicker, though, was listed at the bottom of the rubric: "Because this is a team effort, there will be a team grade. **The whole class will get the SAME grade.**"

This was truly different. In all the years I spent as a student and a teacher, the participation grade was always about 10 percent of the students' overall grade, and it was always an individual grade. A group grade, the thinking went, was unfair because it meant that someone else's behavior could bring your grade down (or up).

But I quickly realized the power of the group grade, which I'll talk about more explicitly in Chapter 6. At the beginning of the year, when I introduced the rubric and the group grade, there was an immediate understanding that they were in it together, working as a team. The grade did not seem unfair because they were not being graded on their individual understanding of the text, but their ability to work together. They were being assessed on how well they approached the text critically as a team, building on each other's ideas and pushing each other to new and better understandings. **Once the goals of *collaborative inquiry and teamwork* were clear to the students, the assessment design seemed logical to them.** However, I don't recommend counting the group grade in students' overall GPAs. I think the most powerful use of the group grade is through symbolic grades that are reported and shared with students and parents through the grade book or reporting systems—but not counted. That is, the group grade is most effective when it is used formatively and weighted 0 percent in overall GPA. See Chapter 6, which is devoted to the assessment strategy, for more information. I believe firmly that using a group grade is the secret to Spider Web Discussion's success. Why? Because we may ask students to work in groups monthly, weekly, or even daily, but unless we provide specific grading or feedback on that process, how do we know if they are learning to be effective collaborators?

I had never considered those questions until working at a Harkness school, but suddenly my mind was bursting with ideas and observations about the process. I began to let go of my instinct to control the class discussion. I listened more and spoke less. Eventually, I began to stay silent during the majority of Harkness discussion time.

I realized then that, for many years before, I had spoon-fed students with the key content, concepts, and questions. I may as well have written on the board every day in class, "Here Is What Is Important in the Text" and added my notes underneath.

Now, however, being in the environment where I was asked to take a step back and empower the students, I realized that students are adept at identifying what is important. It didn't take me long to see that they got much more out of the discussions when they were doing the heavy lifting. It was a humbling surprise and, ultimately, a pleasure to realize I wasn't as important to the process of learning as I believed I was.

From Harkness Method to Spider Web Discussion

In the years since working at The Masters School, I have honed this method into something more detailed and systematic with regard to process, assessment, and self-evaluation. To better reflect the purpose and differentiate it from Harkness discussion or Socratic seminar, I named this specific method of discussion Spider Web Discussion; think of it as Harkness 2.0.

In most high schools, Socratic seminar (or Harkness method) is still driven by the teacher. Although students are doing the discussing, the teacher is still the referee and master of knowledge, offering up the right question at the right moment, redirecting the conversation, correcting misunderstandings, ensuring that students are civil, and grading the participation.

In Spider Web Discussion, the teacher is largely silent. When Spider Web Discussion is taking place in my classroom, I sit in the back, away from the students, and avoid eye contact with them. I have a blank notepad on which I take notes about their discussion.

Who is asking the right question at the right moment, redirecting the conversation, correcting misunderstandings, and ensuring that students are being civil to one another? The students are. That's their job, and I train them over several months to do it. By the middle of the year, they do it very well. I take great pleasure in seeing how irrelevant I become in the classroom about three months into our Spider Web Discussion routine—the students themselves are far better referees and masters of knowledge than we usually give them credit for (or even allow them to be).

The name, Spider Web Discussion, is an acronym that describes all the components of the method:

Synergetic—it's team oriented, balanced, and group graded (the whole class gets a single grade for each discussion).

Practiced—it's ongoing, rehearsed, and debriefed. It's not a one-time activity but a process, much like writing.

Independent—the teacher interferes as little as possible; students run the discussion and self-assess.

Developed—the discussion gets deep, builds on itself, goes "somewhere."

Exploration—this is the main goal; more than discussion, it is a discussion-based exploration (of a text, an Essential Question, or a topic)

with a

Rubric—this is the cornerstone to the whole process: to have a clear, concise rubric against which students can easily self-assess.

The "Web" part of the name comes from the web-like graph that a student or I draw to document the discussion in real time and then we use to debrief.

Spider Web Discussion captures the essence of what the technique aims to do: create graduates who are skilled collaborators, listeners, problem solvers, power relinquishers, and leaders.

What the Research Says

Interpersonal skills are more in demand, yet our education system has not quite caught up. We still largely design our classrooms and lessons—especially in high school and college—for acquisition of academic content instead of "soft" skills.

A 2015 study by an associate professor of education and economics at Harvard University highlights how, since 1980, jobs requiring social skills have grown more than other types of jobs. Especially booming are those occupations that require technical skills coupled with interpersonal skills, such as when doctors or computer scientists work on group projects. The job sectors with the greatest decline were those related to repetitive manual labor, like garbage collection, or individual analytical tasks, such as engineering. Jobs requiring social skills, regardless of the sector, grew 24 percent over the time period the study examined (Deming, 2015).

Our schools need more effective ways to teach social skills, so we can produce graduates truly prepared for their future careers. In 2009, Google began to examine the reasons why people left their company to work elsewhere, and found that one of the biggest factors was having a terrible boss. Google asked itself how it could crunch the numbers relating to who was a good boss and who was a bad boss at an unorthodox tech company. Project Oxygen was born, an initiative that used thousands of performance reviews, feedback surveys, and employee award nominations to distill data points to a list of eight key characteristics in the best managers at the company. Google called this list The Big Eight, and the traits are ranked in order of importance:

1. Be a good coach.
2. Empower your team and don't micromanage.
3. Express interest in team members' success and personal well-being.
4. Don't be a sissy*: be productive and results-oriented.
5. Be a good communicator and listen to your team.
6. Help your employees with career development.
7. Have a clear vision and strategy for the team.
8. Have key technical skills so you can help advise the team.

*Sissy is a term used in The Big Eight Google list.

The Project Oxygen team noted that "what employees valued most were even-keeled bosses who made time for one-on-one meetings, who helped people puzzle through problems by asking questions, not dictating answers, and who took an interest in employees' lives and careers" (Bryant, 2011, BU1). Most fascinating to note is that numbers 1, 2, 3, and 5 all relate to collaborative work or communication. Last on the list is "technical skills." The idea that knowing how to empower a group of people you are leading is more important than your content recall is counterintuitive to how most of us were taught, but it makes perfect sense. In a company like Google, collaboration is how everything is designed, created, and implemented.

Furthermore, Google identified some pitfalls of the company's worst managers, which related to having a lack of management, communication, or collaboration skills. Essentially, if you don't know how to work well within a group, it's highly unlikely you will be successful at your job. In the end, Google was able to use self-generated data on managers to improve business.

A few key lessons are found in the story of Google's Project Oxygen. First, collaborative and communicative skills are paramount, surpassing even technical skills. Second, the lack of those collaborative and communicative skills leads to real losses in human capital in the workplace, an unnecessary loss of talent. Third, feedback is key to the process of leadership; the organization needs employee feedback on the manager's performance followed by specific, goal-oriented feedback on areas for improvement. Basically, Google offers a glimpse into what the real world wants: collaborative, communicative, goal-oriented employees who are familiar with the process of giving and receiving feedback.

It sounds perfectly logically and relatively doable from an education perspective: we want to produce graduates from high schools and universities who are good collaborators, communicators, and feedback givers and receivers. But if these are the skills we want for our graduates, the key question is this one: what are we doing *daily* in our classrooms to teach, encourage, and assess these skills?

We might say that we encourage our students to work in groups all the time, but are we giving them feedback on how well they are working in those groups? Are we assessing the quality of their collaboration? The frequency with which they seek it? How well they communicate with each other?

When we examine the issue more carefully, we see that few of our classes are set up to really teach, encourage, and—most important—assess these skills. If we want students that collaborate well, isn't it logical that we need to teach and assess the skill of collaboration (the teamwork itself) and not just the product (the content or presentation)?

If you are using Common Core State Standards (CCSS), you may have noted that the standards for English-Language Arts are skills-based and not content-based. There is no required list of content, but there are skills standards for college and career readiness, such as "prepare for and participate effectively in a range of conversations and collaborations with diverse partners, building on others' ideas and expressing their own clearly and persuasively" (CCSS, 2010). The beauty of Spider Web Discussion is that it perfectly supports students in attempting to reach that standard at the same time it supports the aims of the businesses mentioned.

The research on the importance of teaching interpersonal skills is clear: we need to design our schools backward from the goal of creating students well versed in collaboration, listening, problem solving, and empathy. I have found that Spider Web Discussion accomplishes this without investing in extensive training or technology. In Chapter 2, I'll introduce the method in detail and explain how to start your first day of Spider Web Discussion in the classroom.

Practical Considerations

Before you begin Spider Web Discussion, it's important to take into account the kind of school, district, and community you work in. Will there be support and enthusiasm from your supervisors? Parents? Students? If you find that the answer is "yes" to those questions, then it will be easy to begin Spider Web Discussion.

If you are not working in ideal conditions, study the lay of the land and make adjustments. At the Masters School in Dobbs Ferry, New York, I was working in a Harkness school, where teachers, parents, and students were all familiar and comfortable with student-led discussions and the assessment of it. When I moved to an international school in Qatar, strict policies required me to teach and assess in lockstep with my colleagues. In that case, I continued using Spider Web Discussion in my classes, but I no longer reported the grades in the grade book. They became symbolic, unreported grades that were discussed with the students. When I moved to yet another school, there was a policy in that school's academic handbook that prohibited group grades for group work. The policy was written to avoid the perennial problem wherein one student does all the work and several other students get the grade without lifting a finger. When I explained that the premise of Spider Web Discussion is different, that it actually grades the process of working together itself, assessing the nature of collaboration and teamwork through a critical inquiry, the principal agreed it was a unique use of group grading. He allowed me to go ahead with the assessment, as long as I informed parents at the beginning of the year. I did that using the course syllabus. During these early years, I advocated for counting the group grades, even slightly. More recently, I believe that using the group grade as a "doesn't count, weighted zero" formative feedback mechanism is more in sync with practices that include grading to standards and avoiding unfair group-grading scenarios. If you explain to students, parents, and administrators that the purpose of the group grade is feedback toward specific goals related to collaboration, speaking, and listening, and that the grade doesn't affect individual GPAs because it is weighted 0 percent, you shouldn't have too much difficulty implementing the method where you work.

Doing a little research on the school policies and getting the appropriate permission from supervisors will help to ensure you don't encounter the unfortunate situation of trying and seeing success with the method, only later to discover that your district restricts it. You should also consider whether your school has a reporting mechanism or grade book that allows for 0 percent weighted grades. If it does, you can enter the group grades for students and parents to track progress, yet keep those grades from affecting individual students' grades. If your school doesn't or can't report in this manner, then you can use the grades in the classroom symbolically, talking about them openly and keeping a record on a chart or clipboard, but not reporting the grades officially.

Another key is your student population. The vast majority of students are thrilled to find they have a valued voice. They feel worthy and trusted when we educators give them the opportunity to take ownership of their learning through a method like Spider Web Discussion. It is always a joy when I observe the first Spider Web Discussion of a school year and students' faces light up with pleasure and engagement because they are allowed to discuss freely and feel intellectually valued by their peers and the teacher.

But there can be resistance, especially with students who are more comfortable being spoon-fed the right answers by the expert teacher. Introducing the method needs to be done more deliberately in these kinds of settings. See Chapters 4 and 5 for more information on troubleshooting different students' personalities in the context of Spider Web Discussion.

The next chapter will help you introduce the method in your classes step-by-step and you'll learn exactly what to do and expect on day 1.

Voices from the Field

—PROFESSOR ERIC MAZUR, DEAN OF APPLIED PHYSICS, HARVARD UNIVERSITY—Many K–12 teachers make the mistake of thinking that colleges want students who have memorized a lot of information or internalized a lot of content, that what high school graduates most need to be prepared to do is listen to lectures, take notes, and perform well on traditional tests.

As a current professor of physics, I can tell you this is utterly false. We don't need good note takers—we need students who can hold ideas up to the light and challenge, question, test, and hypothesize about them. We need leaders who can ask deep questions and leaders who can also sit back and listen, learning from others. Science depends on this process. Physicists, chemists, and biologists work together, not individually in isolation. Scientists consult all the resources and people on hand when they are trying to problem solve; they don't rely on their memory the way we require students to in traditional test-taking. If we truly want to prepare K–12 students for college and career success, we must take the focus off content recall and assessment practices that are outdated, testing only lower-order recall or computation skills (after all, smartphones have these skills!). I used to have very traditional, lecture-based, test-based courses. Over the years, I realized the top performers could not accurately answer conceptual, application questions. There was a disconnect between their high grades and their true understanding of the material.

Now, my courses look very different. They are built around group problem solving, inquiry, and discussion. Not only is class more interesting for the students now, the research also shows that they actually learn more and better this way. Their understanding is way up, their depth of thinking far greater.

Big Takeaway

Today's jobs demand more than content acquisition. Both higher education and the professional world want high school graduates that have excellent critical thinking, communication, and people skills. Karen, the business leader described in the opening vignette, is based on the sentiments of a friend. She was open to hiring inexperienced interns who had excellent communication skills because they were more valuable to her workplace than an experienced insider with average or poor communication and social skills.

Spider Web Discussions are just one way to help students improve communication and social skills, but the method works in all kinds of classrooms. Spider Web Discussion is a philosophical approach that can change your classroom and prepare your students for the challenges of the real world.

2 | THE FIRST SPIDER WEB DISCUSSION

Alec had taught high school English in the Ontario, Canada, education system for nearly a decade. Over the years of his teaching, he had been observed by many instructional coaches and supervisors, and he always welcomed the feedback and the opportunity to grow and become a stronger, more effective educator. He adopted many of the suggestions and structures he learned from his supervisors and coaches, but there was one problem that he was told about continually and hadn't figured out how to solve: Alec spoke too much during lessons, and his students didn't speak enough. When they did talk, it was often because Alec had asked a question.

A lover of literature, Alec infused his lessons with his own enthusiasm, but he had indeed noticed that his students were often bored. He didn't worry too much about it; he knew there was a core group of students who were engaged and even a handful that felt passionate, as he did, and he focused his energy on them. Alec knew not every student was going to love literature, but he thought if he shared his knowledge in an enthusiastic way, something was bound to sink in and perhaps a spark would ignite in some of the students. He felt it was his duty to explain everything in detail, to give them all the information, insights, and tools they needed regarding the texts and authors. How else could he be sure they would "get it"?

In his fourth year of teaching, Alec began working at a new school and was observed by an instructional coach who timed the amount students talked versus the teacher during the lesson, and the data was a wake-up call. Although he had heard the feedback that he talked too much, he had never seen the cold reality of the numbers. He was surprised to see that he had talked twice as much as his students—during a student-led discussion! He knew he needed a different approach, but he was hesitant to give up control of the classroom and the discussion. What if they couldn't do it? What if they didn't get to the most important points on their own? After all, how can students truly run their own in-depth discussions when the teacher is the expert? Wouldn't it just be a superficial "fun" exercise that didn't really accomplish much learning? He was nervous about letting go and allowing the students to speak more than him. How would they learn?

Your First Day of Spider Web Discussion: Designing The Rubric

Perhaps you are a little like Alec—intrigued by the idea of Spider Web Discussion and all it claims to offer, but not sure how it would actually work in your own classroom. Perhaps you are already eager to give it a try. Either way, this chapter is a step-by-step walk through for your first day using the method. I'll show you how to prepare for and how to run the first discussion, no matter your specific aims for your course or homeroom.

Before you have a discussion, you need to identify what the goals are for all of your discussions. Specifically, you need to decide what skills you are trying to bolster in your particular course or class and list them for a rubric. So, the first stage of Spider Web Discussion begins with backward design. You'll need to ask yourself, "What student behavior and learning outcomes do I want to see the students master in our class?" Early on in my work at a Harkness school, I received a rubric from a colleague with a list of skills and dispositions that she wanted from her high school English students. I loved the rubric and use an adaptation of it, shown in Figure 2.1, because it clearly and simply highlights the goals of the discussion.

What matters when designing your rubric is that you identify what you want to achieve during discussions with regard to inquiry, style, and collaboration. Colleagues of mine who have piloted or used Spider Web Discussion have adapted my rubric to their own classroom needs or created one from scratch. Figure 2.2 is an example of a rubric made by teacher Janelle Schmidt

Figure 2.1 **Graded Spider Web Discussion Rubric**

Because this is a team effort, there will be a team grade. **The whole class will get the SAME grade.** The following list indicates what you need to accomplish, as a class, to earn an *A*.

Have a truly hard-working, analytical discussion that includes these factors.

1. **Everyone** has participated in a meaningful and substantive way and, more or less, equally.

2. A sense of balance and order prevails; focus is on one speaker at a time and one idea at a time. The discussion is lively, and the pace is right (not hyper or boring).

3. The discussion builds and there is an attempt to resolve questions and issues before moving on to new ones. Big ideas and deep insights are not brushed over or missed.

4. Comments are not lost, the loud or verbose students do not dominate, the shy and quiet students are encouraged.

5. Students listen carefully and respectfully to one another. For example, no one talks, daydreams, rustles papers, makes faces, or uses phones or laptops when someone else is speaking because this communicates disrespect and undermines the discussion as a whole. Also, no one gives sarcastic or glib comments.

6. Everyone is clearly understood. Any comments that are not heard or understood are urged to be repeated.

7. Students take risks and dig for deep meaning, new insights.

8. Students back up what they say with examples and quotations regularly throughout the discussion. Dialectical Journals and/or the text are read from out loud OFTEN to support arguments.

9. Literary features/writing style and class vocabulary are given special attention and mention. There is at least one literary feature AND one new vocabulary word used correctly in each discussion.

The class earns an *A* by doing all these items at an impressively high level. (Rare and difficult!)

The class earns a *B* by doing most things on this list. (A pretty good discussion.)

The class earns a *C* for doing half or slightly more than half of what's on this list.

The class earns a *D* by doing less than half of what's on the list.

The class earns an *F* if the discussion is a real mess or a complete dud and virtually nothing on this list is accomplished or genuinely attempted.

Unprepared or unwilling students will bring the group down as a whole. Please remember this as you read and take notes on the assignment and prepare for class discussion.

Figure 2.2 **Elementary Spider Web Discussion Rubric**

Group discussion	Not Yet ☹	Sometimes 😐	Usually 😐	Mostly 🙂	Always 😀
Everyone participated.					
Everyone listened attentively.					
Everyone spoke loudly and clearly.					
Everyone stayed on topic.					

Group members:

1.

2.

3.

4.

5.

Coding Key:

I = Interruption
D = Distracted, talking, off task
* = Insightful comment
Q = Question

of Mont'Kiara International School (Kuala Lumpur, Malaysia). She introduced her 2nd grade students to Spider Web Discussion as a way to talk about ethical questions drawn from their reading unit. After the discussion, the students used the rubric to reflect and self-assess. Figure 2.3 shows the rubric that my husband, a former middle school and high school Spanish teacher, adapted to fit his course needs, encouraging greater responsibility among the students for correcting one another's errors.

As you can see, much of the content is the same as the English language arts version, but a few key changes focus on the use of the target language in

Figure 2.3 **Spider Web Discussion Rubric in Spanish 3**

Because this is a team effort, there will be a team grade. **The whole class will get the same grade.**

This is what you need to do, as a class, to earn an *A*.

Have a truly hard-working, analytical discussion in which

1. **Everyone** has participated in a meaningful and substantive way and, more or less, equally.

2. Meaningful and substantive participation implies the construction of complete sentences to get a message across or to form questions.

3. The pace allows for clarity and thoughtfulness, but not boredom.

4. There is a sense of balance and order; focus is on one speaker at a time and one idea at a time. The discussion is lively without being "hyper" or superficial.

5. The discussion builds. There is an attempt to resolve questions and issues before moving on to new ones.

6. Comments are not lost, the loud or verbose do not dominate, the shy or quiet are encouraged.

7. Students listen carefully and respectfully to one another. There is no talking, daydreaming, rustling papers, making faces, using phones, or referring to laptops when someone else is speaking because this communicates disrespect and undermines the discussion as a whole. Same goes for sarcastic and glib comments.

8. Everyone is clearly understood. Those who are not heard or understood are urged to repeat.

9. Students help each other in finding the right words or expressions when someone is struggling to get a message across. Students correct each other when a verb is incorrectly conjugated or whenever there are obvious grammatical mistakes. These corrections are offered in a thoughtful way and with the only purpose of improving the oral proficiency of the class.

10. **Only Spanish** is used during the discussion. If someone is having difficulties expressing an idea, it is everybody's job to ask for clarification or to offer suggestions.

11. Students back up what they say with examples and quotations. Students ask others to back up assertions with proof (if possible). The text is referred to often.

the classroom and the requirement that students help their peers in finding the correct terms or grammar for expression of ideas during the discussion.

These two variations are just to get you thinking about the kind of rubric you'd create to suit your particular classroom needs, whether you are a kindergarten teacher or an AP physics instructor. When you are ready to sit down and make your own rubric, it might be helpful to start with my original ELA rubric, as several of the points are universal and not subject- or age-specific. You can modify the vocabulary to fit the age group or subject. Once you have decided on the items that you want to keep from the original rubric, take a few minutes to think about items that are important to your classroom, subject, or process but are not part of the ELA rubric. It might be a specific school initiative or philosophy, a classroom ethos, or a behavior or skill you have been working on or identify as an area of need for your students. For example, in an ELA classroom one of the most important skills students learn is using evidence (quotes from the texts) to support their claims. As an ELA teacher, I want my students to not only discuss their ideas, opinions, and feelings about literature but also to become skilled at citing the text to support those ideas.

What are the key skills and behaviors in your course or classroom? Once you have identified a list, try to get the rubric to fit on one page. Short and sweet (10 items or less) is the goal with this rubric.

Keep the group grading in your rubric as it is really the keystone to the whole method. Again, the grade is not "counted" and you may or may not choose to report it, depending on your needs and your school's policies. In the last decade, I have experimented with using the group grade, using individual grades, using both, and not using any kind of grade. I can say with confidence that the best results by far come when I use group grades only. I will explain how and why the group grade is so important to the process in Chapter 6, the chapter on assessment. But for now, leave it in your rubric as you begin to draft it and take heart that you do not count the grades for Spider Web Discussion.

In addition, I suggest keeping the points related to effective collaboration, such as avoiding interruptions and requiring equality and balance of voices in the discussions. I will provide more detail on why I think this is fundamental to the success of Spider Web Discussion and for creating strong team players in Chapter 4 in "Roadblocks Early On." I have found that there isn't a single teacher or class I have worked with that hasn't benefited from this item on the rubric. Most teachers and students find it a game changer when they see the results in practice, allowing for far greater levels of participation and balance in discussions.

Your First Day: Choosing the Topic or Text

Now that you have developed your criteria for a great Spider Web Discussion, it's time to choose a good discussion text or topic. It's important to choose something that your students will want to discuss, as the first experience with Spider Web Discussion can make a lasting impression. You can figure out later how best to weave Spider Web Discussion into your unit, but I recommend planning a great stand-alone introduction to the method. You want to spark an enthusiastic, engaged response from your students, so choose something very student-friendly (avoid things like Emily Dickinson's poetry or a brief history of scientific notation). Don't be afraid to look to multimedia depictions of important topics, themes, or ideas that will connect with your students.

I have often used Spike Jonze's short film "How They Get There" (Landay & Jonze, 1997), a thought-provoking interaction between a man and a woman on the street that aims to explain how abandoned shoes "get there." Many students argue about what actually happens in the film and I often use it when introducing or reinforcing the concept of symbolism. The film uses some symbolism in the props, clothing, and music, though they might never talk about this in the discussion (and that's OK because I can circle back to that text when reinforcing the concept of symbolism). The film always sparks strong reactions and often divides the room by gender, making for rich discussion. The short film is available online and runs about three minutes; it is intellectually appropriate for a high school or adult audience.

Another successful multimedia text for older middle school and high school students is Macklemore's music video "Fake Empire" (Lewis, 2009). It deals with the role technology and consumerism play in cutting us off from the world and each other, and it resonates strongly with teenage audiences. I have had success using it as an introduction to Spider Web Discussion. For younger middle school students, I recommend Prince Ea's spoken word video

"Low Battery" for the same purpose and message. For elementary school students, try the two-minute film "Just Breathe," which asks students to reflect on strong emotions and how they can make us feel out of control or upset, and how a simple act of mindful breathing can help us navigate them.

Here are a few other ideas:

- If you are an elementary school teacher, consider reading a gripping story with a conflict at its center to get students discussing the role of the characters, morality, and decision making. You might even pose an Essential Question: "Who is a real friend? How do we know?" or one that engages them on ethical issues: "What does the word 'fair' mean? Which rules feel 'fair' to you? Which ones feel 'unfair'? Why?"

- A discussion about growth mindset and how students feel when they encounter a challenge in a subject at school that is hard for them can be fruitful at any age. Offer a short, age-appropriate video on growth mindset (several are available online). Khan Academy has a growth mindset lesson plan available as a free download on its website.

- In a science, health, or social studies classroom, a hot-button ethical issue connected to the unit of study is the way to go for the first Spider Web Discussion. An article, ad, or short film about the death penalty, stem cell research, Black Lives Matter, body image, or climate change may work well depending on your students' interests, experience, and culture. The key is to know your students and know what they would respond to with interest, regardless of where they fall on the hot-button issues.

I'm a career high school teacher, and it can seem challenging to find texts that really resonate with teenagers. But there are many great videos, films, and articles in magazines and newspapers that get students jumping out of their seats. One of the best discussions I ever witnessed was in my 10th grade English classroom. I asked students to read the teaser for Amy Chua's infamous parenting book *Battle Hymn of the Tiger Mother*, an article called "Why Chinese Mothers Are Superior," from the *Wall Street Journal*. It evenly divided my multiethnic students on how best to raise children and how good a job their parents had done with them. They all declared it the best discussion they had ever had, and it was not related to any other unit—but they were abuzz with excitement from the article. One student was inspired to write his IB Extended Essay, a 4,000-word research paper, on Chua's use of diction to achieve a didactic tone. When in doubt, with teenagers, choose something that speaks to their real lives: critical examinations of power structures in which they feel disenfranchised, such as school, parents' rules, college admissions, or social media trends.

Regardless of age or subject, you might even begin with a well-crafted essential question. The key is to find a question that speaks to students and inspires immediate response. Here are some I have seen used with success in Spider Web Discussions:

- Do parents always know what's best for their children?
- Can a hero do bad things and still be a hero?
- What happened in the past that still influences my life today?
- How do we know something exists if we can't see it?
- Why do people move? (social studies lens)
- Which is the universal language, math or music?
- What if my right is your wrong?

Your First Day: Setting a Time and the Teacher's Role During Discussion

Once you have finalized your rubric and settled on an engaging article, video, or question, you are ready to introduce Spider Web Discussion to your class.

I always do this by first explaining that we are going to try something new, a different kind of method for discussion. I explain to them that they are going to practice sophisticated, high-level skills in collaboration and communication, the kind that big companies like Google look for in potential employees. I explain that it might be different from discussions or structures they have had in the past, and that it is perfectly OK not to have experience with it. I explain that the primary goal is to have such good discussions that they won't want to stop when the bell rings. This, I tell them, is up to them. The energy they put into the discussion will be commensurate with what they are able to reap.

Then I show them an example. I have a 10-minute video of my 9th grade classroom from 2007 (https://www.youtube.com/watch?v=jHi06vm5uJk) that I share with middle school and high school students. It showcases a dozen English students discussing *Romeo and Juliet* by taking turns, writing ideas on the board, and citing the text to back up their own ideas and build on the ideas of their peers. The video is interspersed with individual interviews with some of the students, who talk about what it feels like to be in charge of their own discussions. It's a fairly sophisticated discussion, and this is the point—we want to start by showing the students what we are reaching for in our work with Spider Web Discussion.

When we finish watching, I always ask, "What did you notice? What do you think?" Students almost always say things like, "We could never do *that*." Or, "I can't believe they are only in 9th grade." I make a point to mention that the students were filmed in April after many months of practice with the method. It took until April for them to be that good at it; it looked nothing like that in September. It's important to stress that this is the goal—we are working toward a sophisticated discussion like the one in the film. "I hope, by April, that we too can achieve it," I always encourage them.

At this point, I pass out the rubric in hard copy for all to see and have with them at the table. I love to save paper and try to go digital as much as possible (when I taught, I graded almost all my papers digitally and never had students print them out), but I always hand out a paper copy of the rubric when introducing Spider Web Discussion. First of all, I find in a digital age, paper lends any resource a kind of legitimacy and I want the students to feel the importance of the rubric. It is the foundation for all we will do together in these discussions, and so I want them to have a copy with them at all times. They will need it at the end of every discussion when they self-assess and assign the group grade for the day.

Another reason I don't use the digital version of the rubric is because I have found that screens are anathema to good discussions. I love to integrate technology into my lessons and have worked many years at 1:1 schools where we use apps and laptops or smartphones to facilitate learning, but I have learned that the only way to build a strong, community-based discussion culture in the classroom is if everyone turns off their screens. That rule can be challenging when students are discussing a text and want to reference an online source, so I usually allow a hard copy sheet of quotes, their notebook, or a printout of anything they want to reference, but not their screens. Invariably, someone is distracted and that takes away from the purpose and power of the method. This method is best done unplugged.

Once I pass out the rubric and ask students to read it, I ask them what stands out. Someone always mentions the group grade. I smile and thank them, explaining that this is probably different from other grading systems they have experienced but to think of it like a soccer game—we are all on the same team, trying to score a goal. And they should think of me as their coach in that game, giving feedback from the sidelines, but I am not the star player. We are all in it together. The goal is an excellent discussion. I tell them that, in the future, the group grades will be reported so we can track our progress throughout the year, but that they will not "count." I tell them that today, our first day, will not be reported or counted—it's just a practice grade so they shouldn't feel any kind of pressure.

At this point, we organize the setup of the room into a circle or oval shape so that everyone can see everyone else. Sometimes we move the desks and tables into a circle and sometimes we push the desks against the walls and turn chairs to face each other in the middle of the room. For younger students, making a circle as we sit on a carpet is a great way to begin.

Next, we set a time that is age appropriate and I tell them that they will carry the discussion for the duration of that time. For 9th grade, I usually set it at 30 minutes. For 12th grade, I might set it for 45 or 50 minutes, depending on how "meaty" the assigned text is. For elementary students, I suggest starting with about 10 minutes, depending on the specific age of your students and how you think they will respond to this kind of student-led activity.

I tell them what time we will stop and then I remind them to make sure they try to accomplish everything on the rubric before the time is up.

At this point, I take a chair and move into the far corner of the room where I can see everyone. I quickly write their names in a circle on my notepad that corresponds with where they are sitting and I begin graphing the students' conversation, drawing lines between student names as their discussion moves around the group (see Chapter 4 for illustrations).

During the first discussion, I am careful not to show the students what I am doing. They merely see me off, away from their circle, taking notes. I circle the name of the first student who starts the discussion. When the second student speaks, I draw a line from that first student to the second one and leave it there until the next person speaks, and then I draw a line to that person's name, and so on. The result is a web-like structure of lines that forms the pattern of the students' discussion.

I also write codes next to the students' names for certain behaviors I want to highlight: Is (Interruptions), Ds (Distracted or off-task behavior) and Ts (Text references). I use this data during the debriefing portion at the end of the discussion. For more detailed explanations on how I use coding, see the "Advanced Applications" section later on in this chapter.

Sometimes students are uncomfortable running their own discussions. Mostly I find that students jump right in, but after about 10 minutes during the first discussion, students often have this erroneous idea that they have now "covered" every aspect of the topic. I have seen this happen so often that I recognize it clearly now when I see it; do not be afraid if it happens to you. You might begin to panic, thinking: *What should I do? They have finished their discussion, which wasn't great, and we still have 25 minutes left on the clock!*

I do not, under any circumstances, jump in and save them from their silence. I learned early on not to save them, or the process of building independence (the "I" in Spider) would be delayed or snuffed out. Sometimes the students keep it going the whole time allotted. Other times, there is awkward silence or nervous laughter as they look over to me, expecting me to take the lead. I don't discourage any of this, but I do not engage with them, either. We agreed on the time the discussion would finish, and that is the time we will stick with. If the students are to be independent, effective collaborators working toward a common goal, then they need to work out the kinks on their own. No one has ever died of awkward embarrassment. If they learn how to manage the uncomfortable group dynamics of trying to get everyone in a large group to work toward a common goal, then they must be allowed to traverse all the bumps in that road. What I do while they flounder in silence is allow them their space; I take notes quietly and I avoid eye contact. They always get over that first stumble when they realize I am not going to step in and lead them. Usually around the 15-minute mark, the discussion starts getting interesting. It takes some time to warm up and get used to the dynamics, the awkwardness, and the personalities of the group (some may be chatty and others may be silent). While they find their footing, I continue to take notes silently. I never interject; I never save them; I never add my thoughts to theirs. Sometimes I pretend to look busy and take notes when I am really just scribbling as they stall—no matter. Make yourself look busy and let them take responsibility for their own ideas and collaboration. You will find that for most students, the time flies by and you will have to cut them off when the time is up.

Your First Day: Debriefing After the Discussion

When the time is up, there is usually an interesting web on your notepad, often imbalanced and with lots of lines between the most vocal students. Some students may not have any lines drawn to their names because they did not manage to participate for one reason or another. I stand up, announce that the person currently speaking will have the last word, and make my way with my chair to their circle. I believe it's important to physically join their circle and not to remain at your desk. In this way, you are coming to join the conversation as an equal member, communicating once again that it is a collaborative effort and not the typical teacher-student power structure we are used to. I might summarize some of the discussion or ask them to describe how it felt to be in charge of their own discussion for such an extended period of time. I find they are often quite honest, laughing about how chaotic and messy it was, or acknowledging how painful it was to sit in silence for a few minutes.

I share the web graph with them (it's best on the overhead or interactive whiteboard) by saying, "Here is a map of your discussion." They love to see it and get quite animated noting all the lines emanating from the names of the chattiest students and the lack of lines drawn to the names of the quietest kids. Then they start asking about the letters. "What does 'I' mean, Ms. Wiggins?" one student will venture. When I tell them it stands for "Interruption," they often burst out laughing about how many times certain students interrupted. The web is a powerful visual tool for feedback; it's one thing to say that the discussion wasn't balanced or equal, but it's another to show them a completely lopsided, ugly web. They instantly see it.

Then I ask them to pull out their rubric copies and go down the list one by one and agree as a group whether or not each point was met. In my experience, the students are pretty accurate at assessing themselves. Some points make this easy; to find out whether everyone spoke more or less equally, all we have to do is look at the web. Other points, like whether or not students were digging deep and taking intellectual risks, are more subjective; I do find, however, that the most I need to do is prod them with a little question like, "Was that as good as you guys can do? Can we do better on that point next time?" in order to have them accurately rate their performance on those more subjective points. After they have gone through each point on the rubric, they are able to assign a group grade. Nearly every single time I introduce Spider Web Discussion, someone always shouts out "*A!*" at this point of the debrief. When this happens, I smile and put it back to them. "How many things did we accomplish today on this rubric?" Several students will acknowledge the truth, which is usually that they accomplished around half of the items. "According to the rubric, then, what should our grade be?" Students almost always respond with a more accurate assessment—a *D*, *C*, or *B* range, though I find the *B*s rare for the first time. Most students rate their group discussions as a *C* or *D* on the first day, which is perfectly fine. The discussion is often quite *interesting*, but based on the rubric, we usually still have work to do and a lot of room for growth. My final question is always: Can we do better? If the answer is yes, then it is most certainly not an *A* discussion. I have never had an *A*-range discussion on day 1. Like I said, this is to be expected. I find it takes most classes months to get into the *A* range, no matter what the age or ability level. Effective collaboration and teamwork is slow, steady work.

Once they finish assessing their performance against the rubric, I talk openly with them about my observations and I ask them to share more about how the process felt. I encourage them to talk about the awkward moments or how frustrating it was that one class member refused to participate, even though someone else tried to include him. During the debrief, I treat the talk as if nothing about it is taboo and as if it were everyone's responsibility. I might say, "If Alex is too shy to speak up during discussion, how can we help her? How can we get her in there next time?" Or, "If Jake is always speaking so that no one can get a word in edgewise, what should our plan be for the next discussion?"

This friendly, open approach to feedback doesn't let anyone off the hook for his behavior, nor does it let anyone off the hook for his classmate's behavior. They begin to see they are in it together. The goal is no longer how to be your best individual self but how to be the best team you can be in the game of critical inquiry. This is a real shift in thinking about learning and assessment for many students, but it's one that I think targets some major gaps in how we educate students to become ethical, collaborative thinkers and problem solvers.

The final part of the debrief is a quick question: What should we do differently next time to make the discussion better? Students share a few ideas and then class is over. In the beginning, the debrief is crucial to the method, and I usually allot from 10 to 15 minutes at the end of every discussion for the process. As students get used to the method over the course of the year, the debrief process doesn't need to be as long. Later in the year, we take only three or four minutes to self-assess against the rubric and share observations. Every now and then, I find my class has a discussion that requires more time to debrief at the end, either because it was so rich that we need more thoughtful analysis of it, or because it was a collection of missed opportunities and wheel-spinning that needed my insights and guidance. When those days arise, I try to leave a good 15 minutes for the fuller debrief sessions. But by the middle of the school year, the discussion method and its feedback session at the end are second nature and quite brief.

When I introduce Spider Web Discussion (SWD), the reaction from students is equal part excitement and anxiety about this new way of doing things. Many students love the voice, collaboration, and independence they have in this setting, and many others fear them. The first day can be nerve-wracking or exhilarating for teacher and students alike, and it takes a few days or weeks to feel like you have found your footing. So don't draw any hard and fast conclusions from the first day. Remember, SWD is best used not as a one-off activity and is more like writing, a process that is honed through practice and feedback over many months. See Figure 2.4 for four nonnegotiable principles for SWD.

I do get a little thrill every time I see a teacher introduce the method for the first time and the classroom bubbles over with the excitement at this new, different approach to learning. Almost all teachers report that they heard more from quiet students than ever before and that they were pleasantly surprised

Figure 2.4 **Nonnegotiable Principles for SWD**

Although there are some variations on how to introduce and use the Spider Web Discussion method, here are four nonnegotiable principles:

1. Students must sit in a circle so that they can easily see everyone, face-to-face.

2. The teacher must be silent throughout the agreed-upon discussion time, only observing (unless the discussion is causing emotional harm to any student). In addition, the teacher must sit outside the circle of students, in a chair that is the same or similar to the students' chairs.

3. After the discussion time has ended, there must always be from 10 to 20 minutes allotted for the students to self-assess, provide and receive feedback, debrief the discussion process and content, and set one or two concrete goals for next time.

4. Using clear and easily assessed criteria, the students decide on a group grade and the teacher either agrees or tweaks it based on specific criteria and feedback. This grade should be (a) no-count and (b) recorded in a grade book (where possible).

I do encourage innovation and experimentation with Spider Web Discussion. After more than a decade of experience with the method, however, I feel very strongly that the optimal outcomes always result from a commitment to these four guiding principles. When these principles are adhered to consistently, the class begins to thrive, embodying a spirit of empathy and deep, collaborative inquiry.

at how much students were able to explore and question on their own, without the teacher's "interference." As I say in the footage of the 9th grade English classroom, it can be refreshingly humbling to see how much students can do without you.

What the Research Says

When I present information on SWD at a conference, inevitably there is a question from participants about the effectiveness in helping students learn important material. Many teachers, especially of social studies or English, can see a natural place for this type of discussion in their courses; others worry that it doesn't help support their course aims, which focus on content acquisition. This is a particular concern for many high school teachers in subjects like biology, economics, and history, which focus on "learning" a large volume of content in order to see success on end-of-course exams such as AP or IB.

The first and most important point I like to raise in response to this concern is that education is moving away from considering content as the most important component of learning. We know well from our own educations and from our students' and children's experiences that just because material was taught does not necessarily mean it was learned. For example, I might correctly memorize the definition of the word "surreptitious" but be totally unsure how to use it in a sentence or I may use it incorrectly. I'd ace a quiz on definitions, but I might not actually be able to use the word properly in my communication, which is the point of memorizing the word's definition.

The bottom line is that most of us have acknowledged that basing our students' learning on content acquisition and memorization has never led to mastery for a majority of students; at best it can lead to the appearance of mastery and usually for the students that least need our guidance and teaching to begin with—the self-motivated, high-achieving students. Spider Web Discussion is about taking content, whether it is related to the causes of World War I, cell division, or *Macbeth*, and holding it up to the light to examine, analyze, question, and draw conclusions from it. As John Dewey said in *Democracy and Education*, "were all instructors to realize that the quality of mental process, not the production of correct answers, is the measure of educative growth something hardly less than a revolution in teaching would be worked" (Dewey, 1916/2009, p. 304). I have seen it time and again in my own classrooms and in classes I have observed: the light bulb going off as students' understanding and knowledge of the content is shaped and formed while ideas are being discussed, tested, and sharpened.

The growing research in education bears this out. A 2014 study written by Aleszu Bajak and published in the Proceedings for the National Academy of Sciences of the United States of America (PNAS) compared undergraduate classes in which interactive, collaborative methods were used with undergraduate classes in which traditional lecture was the mode of instruction. The study found that active learning led to an increase in exam performance that translated to an overall average of a half a letter grade. It also found that active learning methods led to a 55 percent reduction in course failure rates.

This study, and dozens more that have emerged in the last 10 years, show what many of us have experienced in our own teaching and learning and what

Dewey so rightly points out: it's critical thinking that sparks true learning, not the production of a correct response. Although content is an integral part of our learning process, it is the means through which we learn, not the end. Spider Web Discussion is a method that can help all teachers guide students through that learning process, grappling with challenging content, toward the goal of mastery and not mere recall.

In my experience, developing a clear rubric is one of the most essential components to the successful use of Spider Web Discussion. A rubric, which is really just physical evidence of group norming, helps the group keep the end goals in mind and allows them to self-assess accurately, creating direction and accountability. As outlined previously in this chapter, the key to a good rubric is to keep its descriptors simple and easy to assess for the age group you teach. Six to eight descriptors is ideal for older students; two to five for younger ones.

Researchers and psychologists are beginning to examine the hows and whys of norming and the role they play in an organization's success. One fascinating example of this was highlighted in a 2016 *New York Times Magazine* article titled "What Google Learned from Its Quest to Build the Perfect Team." It examines the complex mechanisms of successful teamwork, and the article is well worth reading in full for anyone interested in organizational leadership or team dynamics. I will highlight several passages here that help illustrate why some teamwork is productive and some teamwork isn't (hint: the reason has to do with group norms). The article follows the story of Julia Rozovksy, who attended a graduate program at Yale's School of Management and was dispirited by the experience she had in her assigned study group there. She found that her group jockeyed for the leadership position and criticized one another's ideas (Duhigg, 2016).

Rozovsky then looked for an additional group she could join on campus for a more positive experience and found just what she had been looking for in a "case competition" group that worked together to compete for trophies or cash prizes to solve real business problems. Her experience in that group was different and entirely positive. Her case-competition team was fun and easygoing.

After graduation, Rozovsky wound up in Silicon Valley, where group work is the norm. As fate would have it, Rozovsky wound up at Google, assigned to a new initiative called Project Aristotle, whose aim was to study hundreds of the company's teams and figure out why some were successful and some were not. Google must have realized it was on to something big with its Project Oxygen findings and wanted to probe further on the nature of successful group work. One finding the Project Aristotle researchers made was that norms seemed to matter.

It turns out that a previous study, carried out in 2008 by researchers at Carnegie Mellon, M.I.T., and Union College, was the key to unlocking this mystery. This study recruited 699 people and divided them into small groups. They noticed that in the teams that worked well together, members spoke roughly the same amount. When I first read this finding, a light bulb went off for me. Now I had evidence for how important the rubric norm of (more or less) equal talk time was to Spider Web Discussion. Although I always had a gut feeling that requiring students to behave more equally and ethically in their collaborative work had a positive benefit on learning, now there was a study bearing that out.

The next behavior researchers found that all good teams generally shared was equally interesting: the good teams all had high "average social sensitivity," meaning they were able to tell how their team members felt based on their tone of voice and other nonverbal clues (Duhigg, 2016).

This is about empathy—it's about listening and reading your peers' cues to understand if they are nervous, off task, or taking a big intellectual and personal risk. I didn't grasp until I read this article how much Spider Web Discussion creates a space for empathy and inclusion by virtue of its clear group behavior norms. When I watch my students learn to read their peers' anxiety, excitement, or hesitation at contributing to the discussion, they are engaged in a complex dance with each other, reading social cues, acting on them (or sometimes restraining themselves from acting on them, as they gauge a peer's needs).

Finally, the article highlights the key role an empathetic, safe environment plays in a team's success. Google's data showed that psychological safety was crucial to making a team work (Duhigg, 2016).

At the end of the day, we all need to feel safe and supported in order to do our best work; students are no exception. If we focus only on the acquisition of content, we lose sight of what is truly essential in learning: experience and meaning making. Just like adults, students learn more when they feel safe and secure enough in their critical explorations to take risks, ask provocative questions, challenge the status quo, and admit when they don't understand and seek clarification. It's easy to forget how hard this is for us because we don't often find ourselves in the students' shoes. After giving many workshops on Spider Web Discussion and seeking feedback on the experience immediately afterward, adult learners often describe the fear, frustration, or challenge of the group dynamic and assessment. When we design clear norms to help us manage those emotions and experiences, we all grow. This research highlights just how much we can help our students' understanding and growth through effective, collaborative, critical-thinking exercises like Spider Web Discussion.

Practical Considerations

When you begin your first Spider Web Discussion, you'll want to take into account several factors: the classroom space and setup, the students' experience, comfort level, and ability; the number of students; and any specific needs for your students' age and time structure, such as shorter or longer time periods for discussion and reflection. I think the teacher should have a lot of flexibility when it comes to making decisions in these areas, and I wouldn't want to pre-scribe the process too much. The nonnegotiables are the following:

- Participants gather in a circle or oval where they can see everyone face-to-face.
- The teacher provides a clear rubric for students to easily assess their discussion.
- The teacher remains silent and sits outside the circle in a chair through-out the discussion time.
- The teacher debriefs the discussion and its process with the students afterward (5–10 minutes).
- The teacher and students agree on a group grade that doesn't "count."

If you are open to it, it can be helpful to have a critical friend in the room to observe the first discussion or two and to help you graph the web or take notes about what happens during the discussion itself. Comparing notes later and having someone else to debrief with—other than the students—can be bene-ficial. When I observe these sessions, teachers often apologize to me afterward and say, "I'm sorry that was so slow," or "They were so exuberant no one could get a word in edgewise!" or "I know they didn't get to maybe all the content the way I would have if I were leading the class, but I think it was good. Right?" I feel that these responses come from a place of vulnerability about risk taking and letting go. The truth is there is no one way a first Spider Web Discussion should look. I've observed and facilitated discussions that were successful and fun, those that dropped like a lead brick, and everything in between.

Remember this idea: it is a process, like learning to write. You wouldn't declare your 2nd grade students failures on their first writing assignment of the year. You have clear aims and norms for this method, and your goal is to guide the students closer to achieving them consistently by the end of the year. I guarantee that no matter what the results the first time, you will be amazed by the growth as the year progresses if you use it consistently.

Advanced Applications

For anyone who has already tried Spider Web Discussion or is just looking to deepen the level of experience at this stage, coding can be a great way to enhance the process. One of the additions I have developed over the years is to code. It started as a way for me to track things that were on the rubric, like interruptions (something the rubric asked students to avoid) and text references (something encouraged). So I began to write "I" next to students' names on the web graph every time they interrupted and "T" every time they referenced the text.

With time, however, I discovered the power of coding and developed it much more deeply. I expanded the coding beyond the rubric's goals and began to code for other intriguing behavior patterns. For instance, I began starring students' names when they had a really deep, terrific insight that could benefit everyone. In the beginning, I'd star the student's name and write a note about the comment he'd made, and then share that with the whole group in the debrief. Later on, I began using the stars in a more nuanced way, highlighting not only comments that were especially insightful but questions as well. And I began to notice patterns. Some students were especially good at starred comments and some were especially good at starred questions, and often they weren't the same students. Sometimes the ones who asked excellent questions were the students I'd least likely imagine giving a star to—they tended to be more marginalized kids, students who were overlooked socially or academically. Using the coding allowed me to notice that some of the "brightest" questioners (a pretty sophisticated skill) were definitely not labeled as "bright" students.

Intrigued by this kind of feedback, though still not able to really say what it meant to my teaching or grading, I began to expand my coding. I publicly coded for the aspects that I wanted all students to see and share during the debrief, such as interruptions and text references, but I would keep my grade book out during discussions and mark myriad codes for what I saw happening during discussion. The current list of codes I use during SWD is shown in Figure 2.5, though it's always growing; every year I add a new one to the list as I realize I'm seeing a new pattern of behavior I didn't previously have a code for.

Coding has been one of the most interesting aspects of Spider Web Discussion for me, because it allows me to track students' patterns over the course of the year and target them specifically. For example, when Tom has four or five Gs (glib or sarcastic comments) next to his name in my grade book over several weeks, I can sit down and address it with him. I also have a record of that behavior in my book, should it be helpful as a data point during a parent-teacher conference.

Another example is when I noted that a student named Alex spoke a lot but the comments were nearly always given an F code for superficiality, showing a lack of depth or understanding of the texts or ideas we were discussing. After noticing this pattern during a handful of discussions, I encouraged Alex to think through her comments first, or perhaps share some of the deeper insights from her journal, rather than commenting mainly on plot and superficial elements. Tracking the pattern of the kind of comments she made allowed me to see that she wasn't getting deep enough into the texts and that her understanding was weak. It allowed me to target this weakness and communicate it directly to her, all after only a few class discussions and before any major assessments, which come with high-stakes grades. This saved us both time, and it saved her some low grades.

Another student could not speak without getting an R (R is my code for rambling, unfocused, going on and on without a clear, pithy point) next to his name, as his ideas and his arguments were completely circuitous and often just plain off task. After seeing this pattern in my book, I realized staying on topic

Figure 2.5 **Spider Web Discussion Key**

The following is an extensive list of codes that I have developed through years of working with SWD. Most teachers start with 4–5 key codes that are the most common or useful. For me, those are ★, Ad, C, Q, T, and X. Feel free to use or adapt the codes to help you give feedback and track progress during the school year.

1. (Circle name) = Starts the discussion
2. ★ = Insightful comment
3. A = Abrupt shift, cuts off conversation flow
4. Ad = Advances conversation, moves it forward
5. B = Writes on board
6. C^D = Connects to previous class discussion
7. C^L = Connects to life
8. C^{OT} = Connects to outside text
9. C^T = Connects to current text (not reading passage)
10. C^B = Connects to what's on board
11. D = Distracted, talking, off task
12. E = Explanation
13. EQ = Reference to course/unit essential question
14. F = Surface or summary observation
15. G = Glib, silly, or sarcastic comment
16. H = Hard to hear
17. H^C = Asked to speak up
18. I = Interruption
19. IG = Illogical statement or prediction
20. I^{GQ} = Illogical question
21. L = Lost comment
22. LT = Literary term

23. O = Organizing, leading, or calling for order
24. O^H = Asks someone to speak up
25. O^{SP} = Puts someone on spot
26. P = Prediction
27. Q = Question
28. Q^2 = Level 2 Question
29. Q^3 = Level 3 Question
30. Q^4 = Level 4 Question
31. Q★ = Insightful question
32. Q^C = Clarifying question
33. Q^F = Surface question
34. Q^{IG} = Illogical question
35. R = Rambling, unfocused, going on and on without clear, pithy point
36. Rp = Repeating exact point someone else made (didn't hear it previously)
37. S = Reference to author/writing style
38. Sp = Put on the spot by classmate/s
39. T = Reference to the text
40. V = Uses vocab word correctly in discussion
41. V^X = Uses vocab word incorrectly
42. Wb = Graphing the Web
43. X = Error in comprehension
44. X^C = Correction of someone's error
45. Y = Synthesizes, sees big picture

was also a great challenge for him in his writing. I crafted some strict measures for him to follow, such as requiring that any sentence he wrote had to be less than one line in length and that any thoughts he spoke during SWD were to get directly to the point. It took a long time to see improvement, but specific feedback on this bad habit enabled him to grow immensely as a speaker and writer. This student had ambitions of being a politician someday, and I hope this specific feedback will help him improve his speaking skills so he can become a pithy speaker.

These three examples, and many other ones I could cite, illustrate an important concept in education: we often fail to give our students enough feedback. In my experience, this is often because we don't have clear enough systems in place to observe and then communicate that feedback. First I needed to track the students' behavior with the codes. Then, I looked at the data and saw patterns emerge. From there, I could draw conclusions about students' abilities and challenges and target them specifically through direct feedback.

I stumbled onto this feedback mechanism almost by accident—it really started as a way to track whether the rubric criteria were being met. Over the years, the coding became a treasure trove of data on each student that helped me not only see students' weaknesses but also see their strengths, specifically ones that are not usually assessed. One student wowed me with his ability to reference the text perfectly to support his classmates' comments during Spider Web Discussion. He had a knack for finding exactly the right passage that would back up his peers' points and he could often do it quickly. This was an excellent skill when pulling writing quotes in their literary and research papers to support their positions. Although the student rarely contributed his own creative ideas to the discussion, he had a talent for finding just the right support for the discussion points. When I shared this observation with him, he was proud. He hadn't thought of himself as particularly skilled at anything, because he wasn't known as a great writer or active participant and the awareness that talent has many facets helped him become a more competent English student and allowed him to take more risks in his own writing and participation as the course continued.

The coding can help flesh out a student's profile not only for him, providing a greater awareness of his strength and challenges, but also for the parents and the teacher. I've found that even when I struggle to say anything good about a weak student's written work or reading ability, there is almost always a pattern to participation in Spider Web Discussion that can help illuminate the student's strengths. Perhaps she is shy but asks great questions, cites the text astutely, or merely includes others in the conversation regularly, an indication of strong empathy or leadership skills.

I also find that it's sometimes far too easy and cynical to label our students as "good" or "bad" in our classrooms; we often feel that the performance data pretty quickly adds up to a clear picture of what kind of student we have in class. But in my experience, Spider Web Discussion—and the coding in particular— sheds a whole new light on the student and illuminates things I had overlooked or not assessed. It was humbling to realize that often the students who asked the best questions were the social outcasts. What did that mean? Were they just less afraid to go against the status quo because of their social standing? Or did they become social outcasts because they weren't afraid to be critical of the status quo? And could I somehow positively affect the social dynamic by encouraging and praising students' good, critical questioning so that it was seen as something desirable—a skill—and not a trait that isolated them from their peers? I'll talk more about the ethical nature of Spider Web Discussion and its effects on the social group later on in Chapter 7, but the coding has humbled me as a teacher and made me rethink how quickly I peg students as something they may or may not be and how quick I've been to overlook other, less obvious talents that may be lying hidden, waiting to be tapped.

Voices from the Field

—LIAM TRIMM, HIGH SCHOOL ENGLISH TEACHER FROM ONTARIO, CANADA—Spider Web Discussion (SWD) changed my teaching practice. I spent years studying various forms of student-centered educational strategies, but always struggled to bridge that gap between theory and practice. SWD became the bridge as I transitioned from talking at or to students, creating instead a learning environment encouraging student-led discussion that fosters critical thinking and inquiry. In all honesty, I feel my classroom has experienced a level of liberation as ideas are developed and discovered rather than implemented or imposed.

I don't want to give the impression that SWD is unstructured or at risk of being chaotic. The beauty of this strategy is that its purpose is not only to generate discussion, but also to develop appropriate behavior. The SWD technique holds students accountable and the educator's role is to monitor participation for both ideas and respectful behavior. Whole-class assessment places accountability squarely on the students.

As an educator at a school that consists of dozens of nationalities, world views, and cultures, subject-specific student dialogue can be challenging. English is a second language for most of my students, and in some cases a third language. Needless to say, generating conversation can be difficult. SWD establishes a community of learners that is responsible and accountable for each individual's learning. Within this context, barriers begin to erode. Kyle, a new student from China, struggled with his English. Within the SWD learning environment, however, he began to express his ideas more confidently as his peers encouraged him. Confidence then spread to his writing and he continues to improve every day.

I feel that SWD acts as that coveted keystone in education. Finally! A strategy that allows for theory to become a practical reality.

Big Takeaway

In this chapter's opening vignette, Alec had a serious wake-up call when he discovered how much talking he was doing in class. He knew he needed a change. Like many teachers, the models he'd seen in place were fairly traditional: the teacher leading the classroom, setting the tasks, keeping track of the time, providing the feedback, and monitoring student behavior. Letting go of this structure, even slightly, was difficult for Alec because he was anxious about what it meant to release control in a classroom setting. Many of us empathize with Alec and know that we should talk less and allow the students more autonomy. But we're scared that if we relinquish control, the result will be chaos. Take heart in the research from business and education that shows that the best and most permanent learning is experiential and active, and highly successful teams use norms to make this happen.

With big smiles on their faces, dozens of teachers report on their first try with SWD, "I had no idea they could *do* that!" Students can do so much more than we imagine if we can shift our thinking about what understanding means and what our role is in helping students get to it. Playing coach rather than judge as students engage with messy, complex ideas through messy, complex collaboration will create a classroom of highly engaged, empathetic critical thinkers.

3 THE FIRST FEW WEEKS OF DISCUSSION

Marie was a public high school English teacher in a large, diverse district with a large immigrant population. Students came to the school with a wide range of English language ability and education experience from their home countries. Marie attended Phillips Exeter's Summer Humanities Institute, which uses Harkness as its vehicle for teaching how to promote critical thinking in the classroom. She really enjoyed the institute and understood that this type of student-centered learning was far more beneficial to the students than teacher-driven education styles, but she struggled with how to apply it in her own classroom. At Exeter, all students are top-notch. Many students go on to Ivy League universities and speak and read English at a fluent level. The average class size at Exeter was 14. In contrast, Marie's classes were typically comprised of 30 students. Although she wanted to use Harkness in her classroom, she worried how to implement it in a setting that wasn't private or elite.

Whenever I present on Spider Web Discussion, there is always a group of teachers that raise their hands when they first learn the details of the method. "That's great," they say, "but I teach math, and you could never do that in my classroom." They are implying that because of the complex, content-driven nature of a subject like algebra, it would be virtually impossible to conduct class in the collaborative manner that Spider Web Discussion requires. "It's fine for history or English," they say. "But you just can't do that in math."

Actually, it isn't only math teachers. Most often math and biology teachers raise this question in my workshops, but language, elementary, and public school teachers also speak up about their concerns about how to use Spider Web Discussions in their classrooms—without taking away time from teaching content.

First and foremost, I remind those teachers of the research in Chapter 2 and note that just because a teacher covers the content, that does not mean students understand it or learned it. Second, if true understanding and learning are our goals in teaching, then asking students to engage in critical thinking and meaning making with content should be our priority. Students who memorize the rule in algebra that they cannot divide by zero may be helped in the short term when solving equations, but how many of them understand why this is a rule in mathematics? It's a simple question that could be asked during a Spider Web Discussion before starting some problem-solving exercises in algebra class: "Why can't we divide by zero? Discuss for 10 minutes, and feel free to use pencil, paper, or the board. Everyone should try to get into the conversation at least once or twice." Some students will intuitively understand that one cannot divide another number by zero because that means dividing it by nothing and therefore not dividing it into any parts at all. Some students won't "get" the question because they have learned only to memorize rules, and the question doesn't make sense to them. And in some students, the question sparks some thinking, some curiosity. To allow the students to grapple with the idea on their own and test out thinking and analogies is to help them deepen their understanding of math. For instance, you might find during the discussion that a student who already understands the concept or begins to "get it" during the discussion might take out a sheet of paper and tear it into half to illustrate dividing the paper by two (as in "into two parts") to help explain it to his peers. He might then tear another sheet into quarters to show dividing by four, and then not tear another sheet at all to show dividing by zero, illustrating that the rule is merely a logical expression of working with zero or "no" numbers. When students work through this confusion with other students, they will come to understand the topic much more deeply. It will also help them in the future because it will spark thinking whenever they come across the opportunity to divide by zero and remember why it cannot be done. Yes, the discussion will take more time than the 10 seconds it takes to ask students to memorize the rule, but they will gain deeper understanding, saving you and your students time in the long run. As students get into higher levels of mathematics, rote memorization won't be enough to help them understand more complex and elegant applications that require questions, estimates, or counterintuitive solutions.

This chapter will detail what the first few weeks of Spider Web Discussion might look like, but it also aims to convince you that regardless of what or where you teach, there is a place for Spider Web Discussion in your classroom. I like to think of it as front-loading—you invest more time up front with the method, trusting that the payoff with greater student understanding will save you time down the line, producing fewer hours of extra help, low grades, and retakes. I have seen it happen in all kinds of unlikely settings including elementary classrooms, large public schools, and in high school geometry classes. Making time for meaning-making discussions and collaboration once, twice, or three times a week pays dividends down the line that results in much greater teacher satisfaction.

One of the best examples I have seen of collaborative discussion working in an unlikely setting is in Phillips Exeter Academy's math program. For the past two decades, Exeter has used Harkness to teach math. At Exeter, there are no math textbooks. Instead, the faculty write their own problem sets that are scaffolded for complexity for each subsequent year of study. The problem sets are reviewed and revised each year by the faculty and the department makes many of the problem sets available online for interested educators at http://www.exeter.edu/academics/72_6539.aspx. Even more interesting, the students work through the problem sets together. They will come into class and one student will put her problem's solution up on the board, and the students will begin to deconstruct how accurately it was solved, if there were better ways to solve it, and how that problem might connect to previous problems they'd considered. In essence, the students are working together to solve problems—exactly what we hope they'll be able to do as graduates of our institutions (or employees at firms like Google). No boring lectures. No repetitive drill and kill. Instead, thoughtful, scaffolded problem sets that are worked through in teams with teacher feedback and coaching as needed.

Again we come back to Google's Big 8. Yes, technical prowess is important. No one is arguing that we shouldn't teach the content of math, but the real world demands that our students *first* be capable problem solvers, communicators, collaborators, and *then* technically savvy, in order to be most effective. Exeter's math department gets this.

I reached out to the chair of the math department, Richard Hardej, because I was so interested in the school's unconventional approach to math instruction. He agreed to a Q&A and here is an intriguing excerpt:

Q: This is the most common question I get asked when I talk about or present on Harkness: "How do you do Harkness in math?" How do you guys at Exeter do it? Obviously, you have a selective population with which to work—capable and motivated for the most part, I assume. But even then, how do you balance the teaching of skills and content with Harkness and its goals of shared inquiry? What does a math class (or an entire four-year program) at Exeter look like?

A: The focus is on students teaching students. The teacher acts more as a coach or facilitator. Our job is to keep the focus on the problem-sets and to pull students back when they go off on tangents.

We do not use traditional textbooks which often provide formulas and then expect students to "plug and chug" by substituting numbers for variables and then "solve" the equation. Over the last 20 years we have been writing our own problem sets. . . . For example, most pre-calculus texts have a section on the Law of Cosines. It's usually well into the text (for example, in the Brown *Advance Mathematics* text, it's on page 350+) and it consists of a boxed-in formula that provides a formula to find the length of the third side of a triangle given the two other sides and the angle between two given sides. Students simply plug in values to solve for the third side. In point of fact, any student who has studied some simple right-triangle trigonometry and has taken geometry understands this problem.

On about page 7 of our Math 3 (the third course of our integrated math program that focuses on pre-calculus mathematics), the students are given a problem that says, "I can walk down one side of a swamp about 200 yards; I can walk down the second side 300 yards and I find the measure of the angle between the two sides to be 32 degrees. How long is the third side?" A hint is given and the majority of our standard 12-person classes can solve this problem without being given a formula. A couple of pages later, with a number of different concepts studied in the interim, they encounter a similar problem, but with no hint. They solve this one and a day later, they are given another problem, this time with literals (letters that stand for the numbers they were given on the other problems). This includes some challenging algebra, but invariably more than a few members of the class will fully develop the formula for the Law of Cosines. (Wiggins, 2014)

There are two notable ideas that Hardej expresses here; first, that the focus is on students leading students, and that the role of the teacher is one of guide—the teacher prevents the students from getting too far off track and helps lead them to deeper inquiry by asking the right questions. Second, the problem sets are designed specifically for students to understand the material more naturally, leading them to discover the Law of Cosines themselves rather than memorize it from page 350 in the text. This is what real inquiry is all about, but it takes deliberate design, planning, and coaching by the teachers.

Although Exeter's program is large and established and takes place at an institution with students who are high achieving, there are small ways you can incorporate this kind of teaching and learning into your classroom, whether you teach high school geometry, AP physics, middle school Spanish, or the 2nd grade. If you need more convincing as to how this is actually beneficial to your students and not just a nice diversion from the real material and content they need to learn, you'll find many studies in the research section of this chapter. But for this next session, I want to walk you through some of the logistics of what Spider Web Discussion looks like in the first few weeks you begin to try it as a regular feature in your classroom.

Getting Started: The First Few Weeks

In my experience, the vast majority of students who have tried Spider Web Discussion are eager to try it again. In a decade of teaching or observing the method, I'd say that 99 percent of classes ask excitedly when they are going to get a chance to use the method again. When introducing the method, it's best to repeat it fairly regularly so students begin to get the hang of it. In the first weeks after the first discussion, I tend to use Spider Web Discussion for a few classes in a row so that students can quickly internalize the expectations. If I had a class of 10th grade ELA students three times a week for 90 minutes at a time, I'd likely organize two weeks with emphasis on Spider Web Discussion, perhaps dedicating 50 minutes in four or five class periods to the method. There is no rule or one best way to do this, and every teacher has a different timetable, population, and course content to juggle, but if you want to see the maximum benefits, it's best to start off using it more often to gain a level of comfort and consistency early on. Later, you can pare it back to one or two times a week, or even less, as you see fit.

I said that 99 percent of students are usually highly enthusiastic about repeating the method once they have tried it. Every now and then, you'll find a class that struggles right off the bat with this method. Usually, this is a class that tends to have low energy and is reluctant to speak up. The class may have a high number of shy students or one dominant speaker who shuts down productive discussion. I'll help you proactively problem solve with this one percent, as well as other tricky situations that arise. For now, let's assume you have a fairly average class that responds positively to the first discussion.

In the first weeks, the importance of norming the rubric, debriefing, and doing self-assessment is paramount. This is your opportunity to set in place the standards and practices for the rest of the year, much like the routines and rules that are so important to elementary school teachers in the first days and weeks of the school year. I stick to my rules on several issues without exception in these first weeks:

- I ask students to gather in a circle so they can see one another, face-to-face.
- I give an appropriate amount of discussion time and the discussion will always go until at least that time (or over, if time allows and productive thinking is happening).
- I do not speak during the allotted time and I sit off to the side, graphing the web, coding, and taking notes for the debrief.
- I allow 10–20 minutes for every postdiscussion debrief, which sometimes includes continued discussion directed by me.
- Within that time, I allow two minutes for students to pull out their rubrics, self-assess their grade, and then compare it to the grade that I think they merit for the day's discussion.

- In the first discussion, the grade is a "practice" grade, not reported or counted. If I work in a system in which I report the group grade, then I begin to report the grades with the second discussion.

During these weeks, above all else, feedback is the most crucial. You are not only providing feedback to students on content understanding, but also on the process itself. Remember that it's a team sport: if the conversation didn't go well, it's everyone's responsibility to figure out why and to try to remedy the problem. During the debrief, I might say things like, "Michael, excellent questions today. Why did you guys not answer them? Michael had some of the best questions we've heard on this text, but you guys were too distracted by your own comments and waiting to speak to really hear them. How can we do better on that next time?" Or, "Jack, see how Marcus was able to speak up and give us that great insight because you asked for his thoughts? When you speak less, it allows space for more ideas to come through, and we all gain. Did you notice that moment?" Or, "Reshma, we still haven't heard from you yet. What can we do about that? Does anyone have any ideas? What if you start the next discussion with a good question? Bring one to next class to start us off."

The debriefing time is also used to continue the discussion or deepen it if you feel that the students didn't quite "get there." If you are discussing the friar's speech in *Romeo and Juliet* during class and students don't make the link between the speech's musings on how nature reflects the good and evil in humanity and the events and characters in the rest of the play, then you would want to use ample debrief time to coach them through those links using questions and suggestions. Try to avoid explaining or lecturing in this time. Even after you join the table and the discussion, try to remember your role is one of coach, not judge or star player.

Even if students don't "get there" on their own in the first few discussions, don't give up believing in them. Just model the behavior, thinking, and questioning you want them to exhibit and remind them that these are the kinds of connections, insights, and questions you want them to raise in the next discussion. Especially for students who have never been asked to think or collaborate like this before, the process can be disconcerting and it may take them time to adjust and see high levels of success. I tell my students that many classes take three or four months to get their first *A*. Remember, it's a process.

Ideally, during the debrief sessions, you aren't only giving students feedback and deepening their understanding, you are also modeling for how they, too, can give feedback when they become more sophisticated in their collaboration. Although you might not expect or want your students to praise or challenge behavior so explicitly, the ideal Spider Web Discussion classroom puts you out of a job. The students become so adept at collaborating on a critical inquiry of the text, debriefing that process, and self-assessing the result that you are merely an observer. I have had a handful of classes get to this level in the past decade, but I've encouraged all my classes to aspire to that standard. It's empowering for the students and provides them with a framework similar to the one Google highlights in its Project Aristotle work: sophisticated collaboration based on group norms produces exciting and productive outcomes. In the case of the classroom, these outcomes are deeper learning, greater student autonomy, more sophisticated social skills, and heightened self-awareness.

What the Research Says

Encouraging these outcomes through discussion might sound good, but how do we know if the practice of Spider Web Discussions helps students learn better, especially in subjects like math, language, and science? Students need to learn a lot of technical content in these courses, so how does discussion help them learn that?

Dr. Carl Wieman, Nobel Laureate physics professor currently teaching at Stanford University, has dedicated much of his career to testing how different teaching methodologies and technologies help undergraduate science students learn. His Science Education Initiative at the University of British Columbia has conducted dozens of studies, some of which have examined how pedagogical methods influence learning outcomes. A 2009 study coauthored by Wieman and published in *Science* specifically examined whether peer discussion improved learning in a large physics lecture course. In the study, all physics students in a given lecture course were given multiple opportunities throughout the course to test their knowledge on a physics question, using clickers that log student responses anonymously. They then engaged in peer discussion with a classmate near them, and then all students answered the same quiz question again (without receiving any further direct instruction from the teacher or learning the true answer to the quiz question). To test whether true learning of the concept was taking place, the students then took a follow-up question individually (without any discussion with peers); the question tested understanding of the same principles but used different parameters. In this way, the researchers were able to test not only whether peer discussion increased understanding of how to problem solve and correctly answer the first quiz question, but whether it was doing so because the astute peers were merely sharing knowledge with less astute ones, who benefited from the shared knowledge by correcting their answer. The follow-up question, labeled Q2 in the study, allowed the researchers to test whether students were truly learning from the peer discussion and able to transfer that knowledge to a new quiz problem without any peer help, or whether they were, in essence, "cheating" by just getting the correct answer from a more knowledgeable peer without learning. The results showed an increase in student learning through peer discussion; the Q2 questions were answered correctly at a significantly higher percentage than the first question. In addition, of students who answered the first question wrong and then the retake of that question (postpeer discussion) right, 77 percent correctly answered Q2, showing a high percentage of students are "learning" through peer discussion, not merely copying their peers' ideas.

The study found that "peer discussion enhances understanding, even when none of the students in a discussion group originally knows the correct answer" (Smith et al., 2009). This is a surprising and compelling data point—students are learning through peer discussion, even when both of those students initially answered the question incorrectly. Through discussion, they are able to see the errors in their reasoning and self-correct.

Overall, the authors suggest that learning outcomes improve through peer discussion, regardless of whether or not there are students in the group with the correct understanding or answer. They suggest that science instructors not overlook this pedagogical method, erroneously assuming that it is not as effective as lecture or slide show presentations.

This study provides compelling data to support how much peer discussion can help improve understanding in those students that don't already know or understand the material, but how does peer discussion affect the "bright" kids, the ones who already know and understand the material? Isn't discussion ultimately a waste of their time—a means for helping their weaker peers work through the content for better improvement but not a means for the strongest students to improve? Two studies have shown the answer to be no; peer discussion benefits the strongest students as well.

The first built on the study by Wieman and colleagues to examine specific concepts that they had not yet explored. They investigated which presentation mode had the greatest effect on student improvement—peer discussion, instructor explanation, or a combination. The findings were interesting. Similar to the first study, the researchers found that student quiz results improved after peer discussion. But it showed a clear advantage for the strongest students. As it turned out, the strongest students showed the smallest learning gains with the instructor explanation (Smith et al., 2011).

Another study tracked student scores before, during, and after their university course transitioned from an individual to a collaborative learning environment. The results showed a definite advantage in using peer discussion for high-achieving students (Gaudet, 2010). These are just some of the studies that demonstrate improved learning outcomes for science students in a classroom that uses peer discussion, wherever on the spectrum the students fall.

The elephant in the room is that many teachers teach the way they were taught, and for most of us, that was a teacher-centric, lecture-based model. The technology has evolved so that today's teachers use digital slideshows instead of a chalkboard, but the pedagogical principle is often the same. Now studies are telling us we need to head back to the drawing board and push ourselves to vary our pedagogical methods more and introduce regular collaboration and discussion to improve learning outcomes. For many of us, this means stepping outside our comfort zones and trying something a little intimidating, like turning over the content to the students and allowing them to work through it.

Professor Eric Mazur, a professor of applied physics at Harvard University, is no stranger to stepping outside his comfort zone to try something new and intimidating. In his talk "Confessions of a Converted Lecturer" (2013b), he describes the painful process of realizing that his students didn't learn very much during his early years of teaching.

Consider the population: his students were top-notch Harvard students, most of whom had scored a 5 on AP physics prior to university and they had been performing well on his tests and giving him strong teacher reviews. But when he gave them the Force Concept Inventory in 1990 to test their conceptual understanding at the beginning and end of his semester course, he was struck by the dismal results. Most of his incoming students at the beginning of his course were scoring a 23 or lower, meaning they were still Aristotelian thinkers about physics and had not mastered the basic concepts of Newtonian understanding. Mazur assumed, of course, that after a semester of his good teaching, these results would improve. At the end of the semester, however, he was dismayed to see that more than 50 percent of his students still scored as Aristotelian thinkers on the Force Concept Inventory. According to Mazur: "They had not understood the material taught in week two of the course, on which everything else hinges" (Mazur, 2013b). Something just wasn't working in his classroom.

Mazur goes on to cite data from a variety of college physics classrooms, from community colleges, state universities, and Ivy League schools, and shows that regardless of the kind of students or setting, the gain in student understanding is only one-fourth of what it should be. Those of us in K–12 education know that this problem isn't limited to universities; we see it all the time in our own classrooms that students "should" be grasping the material we are covering so diligently, and yet so many of them aren't.

So how did Mazur tackle the problem?

He introduced feedback mechanisms via student clickers and discussion. He realized that two students discussing a physics problem, one of them with the correct answer and one of them with the incorrect one, would quickly work out the right answer because the one with the correct one would easily convince the other student. But what he realized with some surprise is that "Mary," the student with the right answer, would do a better job of explaining why the answer is correct to "John," the student with the incorrect answer, than the professor. Why? Because the professor learned physics so long ago and the understanding was so deeply ingrained in his psyche that he can no longer see or understand the difficulty John has, but Mary can. Mary can call upon the assumptions and errors in thinking that she recently struggled through in order to achieve deep understanding, and so she can explain the hows and whys to John in a much clearer way. That results in John understanding the concept and not just using "plug and chug."

Twenty-five years later, Mazur uses a sophisticated system of feedback and discussion in his physics classrooms, resulting in remarkably improved learning results. He even believes in discussion during tests, a model he calls Peer Instruction, and has the data to support how much more students learn this way. He raises the interesting question as to why, when it comes to assessment, we deprive students of the resources that scientists and thinkers have in the real world when they are solving problems. Why do we deny our students the opportunities to discuss, consult, and search the Internet during the test when they will be able to, or even required to, in their professions? (Mazur, 2013a)

In my experience, these findings in the sciences correspond with outcomes I have seen in humanities and math classrooms. It makes sense, even to the most traditional teacher: grappling with content and solving problems using that content is bound to lead to better learning. The barrier for most teachers, especially in high school, is the belief that there isn't time for application, collaboration, and meaning making, because there is just too much material to get through. We need to move away from this type of thinking, not because we are opposed to rote learning or traditional modes of teaching, but because the research is clear. The brain works best with practical, problem-solving models. Students learn better and retain more when they are allowed interactive, problem-based, and collaborative learning opportunities. We cannot cling to tradition in the face of good evidence; it is every teacher's responsibility to know what leads to the best learning outcomes and to adapt his teaching. This doesn't mean jumping from one flavor-of-the-month method to another; it means being willing to try new, unfamiliar, and perhaps scary things in our teaching in the name of better learning. You might believe your students do just fine with lecture and traditional testing, and the grades they get or scores on the AP or IB exams might indicate that you are right. But could they be doing better? Some evidence exists that tests like the AP are not as effective in predicting academic readiness or success as previously thought. Dartmouth College stopped giving credit for AP exams based on their own studies showing that AP psychology exams were not an accurate predictor of success on year-end course exams (Tilsley, 2013). More important, though, is the question of whether grades and scores on exams like IB and AP accurately reflect the crucial "soft skills" so needed by students to make themselves marketable. In the face of studies like those cited here, we need to have an honest conversation with ourselves and within our school communities about what is best for students and their futures. All teachers should be asking their students to practice and get feedback on key skills like teamwork, leadership, and communication.

Practical Considerations

What might it look like in a variety of classrooms? How might you use Spider Web Discussion in an AP biology class or a 2nd grade social studies unit? Here are four specific classroom examples for an AP or IB science course, a large 8th grade ELA class, 2nd grade social studies, and a high school statistics course. Even if your level, subject, or setting is not specifically reflected below, you might begin to get ideas for what Spider Web Discussion could look like in your own classroom or school based on the variety of examples here.

IB Nature of Science

If you are struggling to imagine how to use discussion in your science classroom, the easiest point of entry is to discuss controversial or ethical issues in the news, such as bioethics, climate change, abortion, drugs in sports, genetically modified crops, or vaccination. Students may have heard of some of these issues and the nuances surrounding them, and reading articles about, for example, whether Earth is warming more this year due to El Niño or to greenhouse gasses. Exploring the science behind each phenomenon could produce rich discussion, especially if students are required to read a variety of texts and cite them frequently during discussion. Chris Watson uses Spider Web Discussion in his IB Diploma course Nature of Science, a two-year science course for high school juniors and seniors that incorporates biology, chemistry, physics, and earth science into one integrated course that examines how nature affects our lives.

One of the course's first units is focused on geology and plate tectonics, inspired by the Big History Project's approach to the planet's physical development. Chris's unit has students design an investigation, create a model, and do independent research to better understand how the continents were formed and how those formations have affected people's lives, both socioeconomically and environmentally over time. Once the students have carried out the investigation, modeling, and research, they make meaning of their knowledge through Spider Web Discussion. One of the highlights of this unit is the discussion on the topic: "Which is the best continent?" Students are assigned a continent to research from a variety of lenses (i.e., geologic, economic, environmental) and they defend "their" continent as the best continent during the discussion.

I have observed some of these discussions in Chris's classroom and the energy and enthusiasm is high. One wouldn't expect high school juniors to be sharing data on Antarctica and oil drilling with the passion of sports enthusiasts, but all students were engaged and drawing from a wealth of data to passionately discuss Earth's continents.

Chris is clear that his objective for the discussion is that students come to their own conclusion that there really is no "best" continent in the world. He also wants his students to think carefully about what makes a great continent in the first place. Drawing from the science they have studied, Chris wants them to consider how their assigned continent arrived at where it is today based on plate tectonics, what kind of natural disasters it has endured, and what resources it contains, ultimately leading to the notion of sustainability. For example, students begin to ask "What is the most polluted area of the world?" which leads them to the link between high amounts of pollution and a high volume of coal available in a region. During discussion, students debate various data culled from their research, such as natural resources, disasters, population, and climate to answer the discussion question "What is the best continent?"

The discussion is enhanced by questions that Chris has created or adapted from the Big History Project:

- What landforms, plant life, and animal life are unique to your continent?
- What plate boundary disasters does your continent encounter the most often?
- What current events are there right now from your continent relating to space, geology, environment, and humans?
- What cultural influences are there in your continent?

The "best continent" discussion usually lasts about 30–40 minutes, which allows enough time for 22 to 24 students to fully explore the topic.

Chris describes the notion that discussion has no place in a rigorous science classroom as totally false. "They learn about the scientific method and model making, but the students get very passionate about 'their' continent during the research and discussion phase of the unit. It becomes very personal, which brings to life the science and generates far more engagement and ownership. I still hear about this unit now, in the students' second year. Those discussions make a lasting impression on them and help them connect the material and concepts to the rest of the course, as well as to global issues, which can potentially inspire them to some kind of action-service."

Obviously, in a traditionally content-heavy course like an IB or AP science course, there are units where you feel you have more or less time for a method like Spider Web Discussion. But I think you will find, as Chris did, that students' scores were not adversely affected by shifting time away from pure content delivery toward more meaning making. In fact, several students were able to perform at higher levels than usual due to deeper understanding and curiosity sparked by the questions and collaborative time.

Middle School English Language Arts

Let's imagine that the teacher of a large middle school language arts class wants to use Spider Web Discussion to teach a nonfiction unit. The best way to have successful Spider Web Discussions in ELA and English classrooms is to choose engaging books. I was an English major and I have an MFA in writing fiction, so I am a lover of literature. But when it comes to teaching, I believe that most high school students will learn more and be more engaged in the act of critical thinking if we choose to teach kid friendly, engaging texts, such as a graphic novel like *Persepolis* over a classic like *Pride and Prejudice*. This is my personal bias and should in no way put you off from teaching Jane Austen if you have had great success with it in the classroom. But I'd bet that if you taught both texts, you'd find students more engaged in the skills and analysis you want to see as the end goal with a more modern, engaging read because it's visually arresting, speaks to their own lives as teenagers, and is a peek inside a country (Iran) and at a religion (Islam) they hear of a lot but perhaps don't have much exposure to.

So if I am teaching a unit on nonfiction in a large 8th grade ELA class, I'd start first with essays and blogs that are current, kid friendly, and relevant to the students' lives. I have successfully taught two essays that always spark fantastic Spider Web Discussions. The first is "Why Chinese Mothers Are Superior" by Amy Chua, an excerpt from her controversial book *The Battle Hymn of the Tiger Mother*. The essay was published in the *Wall Street Journal* and is available free online. It's a highly opinionated account of how best to parent in order to raise successful children, drawing from Chua's own Chinese background to make her case. In a large class of students, especially a group that has international or immigrant populations, this one is bound to strike a nerve and produce a lot of spirited discussion. You need only assign the text, set an appropriate amount of time (for 8th grade, perhaps 25–30 minutes as a start), and review the rubric, which should include citing the text regularly to support opinions and ideas.

The second text I have used to great success with young teenage English students is any of the dozen articles on Abercrombie and Fitch's CEO's statement that his company's clothing isn't for "fat chicks" and that its target audience is thin and beautiful people. His 2013 remarks caused a firestorm in the press and a backlash on Twitter and blogs. You might even pair one of the articles detailing his statements with a blog that responds to him, such as "An Open Letter from a Fat Chick to Mike Jeffries, CEO of Abercrombie and Fitch," by Amy Taylor, published on the *Huffington Post*. Students, especially girls, have visceral responses to the way a popular brand of clothing is marketed for (or not) a specific target audience like them. You can even introduce business or marketing ethics into the lesson by including a few questions in your debrief: "What should be done when a remark like this is made by the head of a popular company?" "Is a boycott warranted?" "What choices do you make when you purchase your own clothing?" "What do you know about the brands you buy?"

In a large class, with material that will spark animated discussion, you might want to split the group in half and run a "fishbowl" style Spider Web Discussion (see the "Advanced Applications" section.) But with texts like these, the discussion is pretty much guaranteed to be lively on its own. During the debrief or later in a follow-up lesson, you can use the engaging articles to ask the students questions about nonfiction or essay craft, such as:

- How do these articles hook you? What specific technique or language do they use to hook the reader?

- What role does a title play in hooking the reader? How interested would you be as a reader with a much more academic or general title, such as "The Most Effective Way to Parent"?

- What role does diction play in hooking and engaging readers? What kind of diction is used in these articles and how? What does a word like "superior" connote? "Fat chicks"?

- Highlight topic sentences where you see them. Where are they? Does every paragraph begin with an actual topic sentence? Why do you think that is?

As in the biology example, the aim is to hook students with engaging presentation of content and then have them probe that content more deeply. It isn't enough for them just to read a good essay; you want students to understand why the article is engaging and how they might transfer those techniques to their own writing, so you will want to make those links explicit in debriefing or follow-up lessons and discussions.

2nd Grade Social Studies

One of my favorite examples of using Spider Web Discussion was a classroom lesson I observed at a public elementary school in rural Pennsylvania. The teacher, Shannon, asked her students to conduct a discussion on Dr. Martin Luther King Jr. based on books they read. Shannon set the tone of the discussion by asking the students to think about everything they knew and learned about Dr. King and posed a few questions and ideas. For the SWD, a handful of students sat in an inner circle to discuss the texts and the other students sat in an outer circle and observed. Shannon gave cards to several students along with instructions to hold up the cards based on rubric criteria that is set for all discussions in her classroom. For example, a listener holds up an "off topic" card when a speaker strays too far from the topic or a "listening" card with a drawing of an ear when a student interrupts, talks too much, or needs to listen to others. This explicit link to the rubric criteria helps to keep the students on track and, later, to accurately self-assess as a group. I watched very young students grapple with complex ideas related to race and violence, raising questions, and citing the texts—all on their own. In the debriefing that followed, students talked about how it felt to talk about a topic as a cohesive group in charge of their own discussion, and several students mentioned how comfortable they felt with their own friends there to support them and give them ideas.

If you are interested in using SWD in an elementary classroom setting, I urge you to adapt the method to your students' needs just as Shannon did. Begin by explaining the process of the discussion to the students, laying out the criteria for a good discussion, and encouraging students to ask their peers for details, to pose questions, and to support their ideas with quotations and support from the texts. If you feel your students would benefit, you may assign roles, ask them to write one question on an individual whiteboard before the discussion, or ask partners to think of a key idea or takeaway that they can share in the debrief. Spider Web Discussion isn't just for middle or high school students. It has been successfully adapted to and carried out by all ages and ability levels.

High School Statistics Course

A unit or course on statistics offers great opportunities to use Spider Web Discussion in the math classroom. In 2016, I worked with international school teachers David Lawrence and Adam Cross to design a unit on descriptive statistics that explores measures of central tendencies based on a unit my father spoke of in a keynote speech he gave at an IB conference (Wiggins, 2012).

Adam, David, and I designed backward from the outcomes they wanted for that particular unit:

Students will know the following content:

- Classification of data
- Measures of central tendency (mean, median, mode)
- Measures of dispersion
- Frequency tables
- Box and whisker graphs

Students will develop the following skills:

- Distinguishing between discrete and continuous data

- Graphing:
  - Cumulative frequency curves
  - Histograms
  - Box and whisker graphs
- Distinguishing inter-quartile ranges within cumulative frequency curves and box and whisker graphs
- Calculating mean, median, and mode
- Communicating clearly the relevance of the data analysis students do

Students will grasp the following concepts:

- Sometimes mean average isn't the most "fair" when averaging numbers
- Numbers can be presented in different ways to produce a desired effect on the intended audience
- Numbers themselves don't lie, but the person interpreting them may be skewing them for a specific effect

Given these goals, we worked out a series of essential questions to frame the unit with, based on the criteria of Grant Wiggins and Jay McTighe in their book *Essential Questions*.

Are my essential questions:

- **open-ended**? (as opposed to having a single, final, and correct answer)
- **thought-provoking and intellectually engaging**, often sparking discussion or debate?
- ones that **call for higher-order thinking**? (e.g., analysis, inference, evaluation, prediction, and not mere recall)
- ones that **point toward important, transferable ideas** within (and sometimes across) disciplines?
- ones that **raise additional questions** and spark further inquiry?
- ones that **require support and justification**, not just an answer?
- ones that **invite being asked and re-asked** throughout various points in the unit/course for deeper reflection and understanding? (McTighe & Wiggins, 2013, p. 3)

Adam and David devised the following essential questions for their unit on descriptive statistics:

1. What does "averaging" mean?
2. How do I know if these numbers are misleading?
3. Why do we use graphs?
4. Do numbers lie?
5. How can I intentionally mislead people with the presentation of data?
6. What's fair? What's accurate?
7. What's the fairest way to calculate your grade?

A bookend discussion approach to this unit would be an excellent way to use Spider Web Discussion, asking students to discuss the answers to some or all questions before beginning the unit and again at the end but prior to the final assessment. The last question, "What's the fairest way to calculate your grade?" makes for a riveting student discussion by itself. Is a mean average the most fair? Is a median more fair? Or is it most fair to take only the most recent grades as the best indicator of what students know and can do well on their own, without scaffolding, hints, or prompts? These are all real questions being debated in education today, and they directly affect students' learning and transcripts. This question produced passionate pleas from the students that the fairest way to calculate their grade was to always give them an A, which raises an interesting philosophical question: what does "fair" mean? Many young people erroneously believe that "fair" means whatever they most want (in this case, an A). But that cannot be the definition of "fair." Getting to the bottom of what "fair" means through problem solving, punctuated by a series of Spider Web Discussions, delves into math that actually matters to our students as they learn good numeracy and collaborative skills. There are endless variations and paths for discussions on just that question of fairness in grading; students might even follow up a discussion with a project in which they design a grading system that they believe is more fair than the current one, given a shared working definition of what "fair" means.

Another way to use Spider Web Discussion in this unit is to design a collaborative statistics activity like the one Adam created. He asked students in pairs to read two anonymous political speeches and count the number of words used in each sentence, creating a graph measuring the frequency of sentence lengths for each candidate. Adam handed out two one-page speeches he'd found without identifying the speakers. Right away, students were able to see the stark difference between the number of words used by one author and the other, and by how frequently one author repeated words. Several students guessed Donald Trump was the author of one of the speeches but none of them guessed Ronald Reagan was the author of the other; most students assumed it was Barack Obama.

An activity like this could be followed with a Spider Web Discussion in which students discuss their findings as well as the connections to the content and the essential questions. How do the graphs differ? What do we think that says, if anything, about the speakers? Essential questions like "Why do we use graphs?" and "How could this data be used to intentionally mislead people?" could be reconsidered during this 20–25-minute discussion. Follow-up questions or activities might result, such as tracking and graphing the variety of words used by the speakers and what effects of speaking one way versus another might have on political polls.

There is practical, sophisticated math being used in these types of lessons, but bringing in relevant, real-world examples to discuss and debate serves to hook students into a subject that is traditionally unpopular or even feared. Practical, collaborative math applications can make the subject come alive for students who might not already be naturally inclined toward math or who may not yet understand how it intersects with other fields, like politics or psychology.

Advanced Applications

In the opening vignette, Marie worries how to make Spider Web Discussion work in a large classroom, and this is a primary concern of teachers who don't teach at places with fancy round tables and average class sizes of 12.

In my experience, the number of students for ideal Spider Web Discussions is somewhere between 13–18. I find that in a high school classroom, those numbers tend to lead to the most comfortable, flowing, and productive discussions. However, I have successfully carried out single Spider Web Discussions in classes of up to 24 students, especially in a block schedule system (classes of

80 minutes or more) where there is time enough for all students to get into a good hour-long or more discussion. Once you get beyond 24 students, it becomes increasingly challenging to have a single group discussion. In these instances, I recommend breaking the class up into a fishbowl-style discussion—one circle of students discussing the topic and one circle of students surrounding them observing, listening, taking notes, and giving feedback in a 1:1 design so that everyone on the outside has a specific task. In an 80-minute block, you can conduct two 40-minute discussions for older students, either on the same topic or text, slightly nuanced aspects or questions, or entirely different topics or texts.

Another option is to have "A" and "B" discussion groups and alternate days, so that on Monday the A group will have their discussion while the Bs work quietly on something else or observe in a 1:1 outer circle, and on Tuesday vice versa.

I have run two simultaneous discussions in my class, but I haven't had great success with it overall. It's hard to follow the discussions and bounce between them fluidly. I do know some other teachers, though, that have found this a successful method for their large classes, especially with mature students who don't need a lot of behavior monitoring.

For those high school teachers teaching in short periods (e.g., 45 minutes), high-quality Spider Web Discussions can be more challenging. I recommend trying several approaches and settling on the one that seems most comfortable for you. Perhaps devote one or two days a week to the method and have students arrive in class fully prepared, with the understanding that no other business will be dealt with on those days so as to maximize the full period for discussion. Or perhaps you design longer discussions broken up over two periods. I have tried both of these strategies successfully when I wasn't able to teach during a longer block.

There isn't one ideal way to run Spider Web Discussions based on numbers, time, or space; the best way is going to look different for every classroom, teacher, and group of students. I encourage you to troubleshoot ways to adapt the method to classes that are bigger than 22 or 23 or during less-than-ideal schedules and figure out what works best for you and your students.

Voices from the Field

—NELLIE BRIDGE, ENGLISH TEACHER AT SEQUIM HIGH SCHOOL, SEQUIM, WA—Using the Harkness method, or Spider Web Discussion, with large classes in the public school setting is possible! What I needed to begin was a belief in the method, confidence in my students, highly structured procedures during discussion, and in-class preparation that includes reading, annotating, and developing good questions. My extra support was a piece of furniture that changed the physical space: a portable, folding oval tabletop that sits on a handful of desks and can be comfortably surrounded by 10 to 14 chairs. The table signals a ritual change in task, tone, and approach. Because my classes have 25–35 students, not all of them participate in SWD at one time. Some participate; some observe; none knows ahead of time.

Participants receive a base grade for the group's performance, which I may adjust to reflect individual participation that helps or hurts the conversation. Observers around the table fill out standard forms for an individual grade. At the table one empty stool is a "hot seat," which observers may take to share one burning question or comment.

Listening to my students' conversations, I gain new insights into our texts and am consistently impressed with their sensitivity and politeness to one another. Throughout the year, we reflect. Many students suggest practical changes, and report that they love it—they enjoy getting their ideas out, build confidence by expressing their ideas, learn from one another's perspectives, and come to new understandings of the texts. I hope the culture born of the conversations also extends beyond my room, to increase the friendliness and thoughtfulness of the broader social culture at the school.

When I was teaching in a small, rural, west coast city, I realized that many of my students had not heard of boarding school or specialized high schools. Most were not used to participating in a discussion in which they were responsible for leading and facilitating the conversation. To introduce the method at the start of the year, I explain the history of the Harkness table at Phillips Exeter Academy. I wondered if my students, many of whom live in poverty, might enjoy the fact that they can use the same methods as students with access to greater advantages. I discovered that these introductory materials have been more useful to clarify expectations and as concrete examples of other students doing it well. My students do not seem motivated by the differences in class or privilege. They don't perform well in discussion because they are trying to keep up with private school students. They perform well in discussion because they are capable of it and because it is natural to want to participate and contribute to a shared inquiry—to try things out, explore, and be part of the conversation.

I value the physical presence of a table to signal a certain kind of endeavor and attention, but you don't need a table or a tabletop. If you're starting this practice alone in a public school classroom, you may need to invent work-arounds for various constraints, but mostly you need just a belief in the method, and a belief that students can do it.

Big Takeaway

As we saw in the vignette at the beginning of the chapter, a teacher like Marie had real concerns about how a method that developed out of an elite, small, private setting translates to a big, inclusive public one. Both Nellie, in the above testimonial, and university professors like Eric Mazur show that "where there is a will, there is a way."

A high school math teacher who attended one of my workshops wrote to tell me that using Spider Web Discussion with her geometry class gave results that were "better than expected." She noted: "It's a wonderful change in the way I 'don't teach' my students." I have heard this story numerous times—skeptical workshop attendees who teach math, science, elementary, or in large public school classrooms try Spider Web Discussion and report being pleasantly surprised both by increased enthusiasm and better learning results.

If you are worried about what your colleagues or administration might think if you want to introduce discussion into a classroom that typically doesn't "have time for that," share Mazur's talks or Wieman's data to convince them it's worth trying.

4 ROADBLOCKS EARLY ON: SHY KIDS AND SUPERSTARS

Vanessa was a top student, excelling in dance, music studies, and academics, and was respected by her peers for her thoughtful insights during class and social time. Vanessa enjoyed talking and found that people often enjoyed listening to her. She sensed that she had a certain ability to think and question that she didn't see as often in her classmates, and she liked the feeling she got when her parents, teachers, or peers commented on how bright she was. She secretly prized those moments when teachers would look surprised and remark something like, "Wow, Vanessa. I hadn't even thought of that. Excellent insight." She saw something like pride reflected in their faces, and she, in turn, felt pride.

Most of the students in her classes, save for a few like her, did not talk much. She figured if they had something insightful or important to say, they would speak up. If they didn't, then they likely didn't have anything to share or already agreed with what she and others were saying. Vanessa was happy that teachers seemed to like her, and she always got top marks for class participation.

I've discovered that most students love Spider Web Discussions. I'm always surprised by the reaction, year after year, when I introduce it to new classes. Within the first few days and weeks, there is a palpable feeling of challenge and excitement; the dynamic shifts, giving students more control and encouraging camaraderie.

Some students, however, are wary of this new approach. I find that these reluctant few nearly always fall into one of two categories: the shy, reticent student, and the bright, talkative student. Both of these kinds of students feel that the dynamic has shifted in a way that penalizes them for being who they inherently are. You will recognize them right away in your discussions as the ones who struggle the most with this method. I do not mean to imply that all students who would describe themselves as shy or those who are bright and talkative will balk at Spider Web Discussion, nor do I mean to disparage either of these kinds of personalities with general terms. Rather, the terms "shy" and "superstar" are affectionate generic descriptions for the kinds of students who struggle to find their footing with Spider Web Discussion. These kids have grown comfortable with the system and status quo and do not like disruption. But sometimes disruption is just what we need to realize our greatest potential.

In most secondary schools, shy and reticent students have learned that if they just stay quiet enough, most teachers will not call on them and the superstars gladly fill the discussion space that they leave empty. They have also learned that this doesn't usually affect their grade detrimentally. In high school, a common percentage allotment for a participation grade in a course like English or history is 10 percent, so even top students can participate rarely or never and still get high grades overall if their other work is done to a high standard. We all know students like this—the quiet, studious, insightful kid who might wow us with her moving personal narrative on the page but will never open her mouth during discussion unless she absolutely has to, and sometimes not even then. And all teachers have experienced those uncomfortable moments when we call on a student to contribute or give the answer and he freezes up, flat-out refuses, or mumbles "I don't know." Often, we feel so much empathy for the student that we move on and call on a student who will happily participate. I used to do this all the time. I felt that I was asking the truly shy students, the ones for whom talking seemed painful, to do something they were incapable of. I now believe I was wrong.

Think about a typical class discussion, no matter what age or subject you teach. The discussion usually organizes itself by a predictable pattern—superstar students will lead the way, usually by offering up ideas or commenting on others' ideas. Many times these superstars' ideas are insightful and contribute both quantity and quality. Quieter students will mostly listen, occasionally add something, and will tend to stick to the sidelines and let the discussion carry on without them. They are spectators in the act of shared inquiry, which right away alerts us to the idea that perhaps the inquiry is not quite as "shared" as it could be. In between the superstars and the shy kids are a few voices that sometimes get heard and sometimes get drowned out or cut off by the superstars. Superstars aren't usually rude or ill-intentioned in drowning out others' voices, but their own excitement can easily dominate and take up all the space so that quiet students tend to hold back.

In traditional models of class participation, we reward superstars for their behavior. Before I developed Spider Web Discussion, I rewarded those students with top marks for participation. They were, after all, participating often and of their own volition. They seemed like good models of participation. My comments to shy and moderate talkers would often read something like, "I continue to encourage Sarah to speak up during class discussions, as we could all benefit from her insights more often." But these comments never had any effect on students' behavior. The reticent students had already decided that they weren't able to be active participants, and they allowed their louder peers to play that role.

Everything changed when I began to think more deeply about what makes a good discussion, thanks to the rubric I was given at the Masters School. What did effective participation really mean? What did it look like? Ultimately, it was a question of backward design: if I designed backward from what makes for a great discussion, what would I need to see and assess? Framing it this way made the answer clear: neither the shy kids nor the superstars were helping us meet our goals, which were based on balanced (more or less) participation, building on each other's ideas, and taking risks. Although it was immediately evident that the shy kids weren't helping us reach our goals because we just weren't hearing from them, it was less clear initially that the behavior of the superstars was a problem as well. A closer look revealed the truth: these students were dominating the conversation, not allowing others to get a word in edgewise, assuming that everyone always wanted to hear their opinions, waiting to speak rather than listening, and interrupting. I realized then that I had been giving students As for bad behavior—that they were unconsciously acting as discussion bullies.

I don't mean to be hard on the superstars. I confess that I am one myself—a naturally social, verbal, and participative person. I loved participating in classes throughout my education, and I'm certain that I was one of those students most of my peers wished would just shut up (I probably still am!). It was actually much harder for me as a teacher to understand the reticence of my shy students, because I could never imagine not wanting to speak. I was always so excited to partake in the exchange of ideas that I had trouble understanding what held shy students back. So, as a self-confessed superstar, I will be honest: too often we teachers not only give superstars a pass for egocentric behavior during discussion times, we actually reward them for it. Spider Web Discussion works as an equalizer—it asks the shy kids to pull their weight and it encourages superstars to be true discussion leaders.

The shy students and the superstars have to negotiate this new terrain and it initially makes them uncomfortable. I talk openly about this and how it's hard for quiet and loud students alike. I don't ignore the elephant in the room. Instead, I keep reminding them that the goal is to have the best, deepest, most interesting exploration of an idea we can as a team. How can we do that if only a few people are involved?

The hardest class I ever had with regard to making Spider Web Discussion successful was at an international school in Malaysia in 2012. I taught four sections of grade 9 English that year and one of them, E block, was an anomaly: nearly all the students in the class "hated" Spider Web Discussion. The luck of the draw that year led to a class filled with shy kids. About 80 percent of the class was hesitant to say anything at all during discussions. The vast majority of the students in that class were Malaysian, Japanese, or Korean. For many students from these cultural backgrounds, speaking up, relying on a student-led method, or disagreeing with peers' or the teacher's ideas can feel uncomfortable and even ill-mannered.

When I first introduced Spider Web Discussion, there were a few students in the class who were conscious of the group grade and wanted to score well on it (at this point in my career, I was still counting group grades, so there was more anxiety about it), so they decided to facilitate discussions. The first day we tried it, Gown began launching questions to the group in rapid fire. One of her more participative peers would respond, and then that line of discussion would die out. Gown would then fire off her next, unrelated question, and another student (or the same one) would respond briefly to that question. This went on for about 20 minutes. It was a disaster. Figure 4.1 shows the graph of that first day.

Students like Kevin, Jason, and Sua only spoke because they were put on the spot by their peers through specific and direct questions, but it was obvious they preferred not to participate and were highly uncomfortable. The whole first day—an excruciating half hour—was a flop.

I never worry when the first day is a flop. Spider Web Discussion is a new way of running class discussions and it takes a good deal of adjustment. So, during our debrief, I tried to openly address the awkwardness during that first discussion, how hard it could be when a few people dominate and others say nothing unless called on. I asked them what could be improved, and they

Figure 4.1 **E Block First Discussion Disaster**

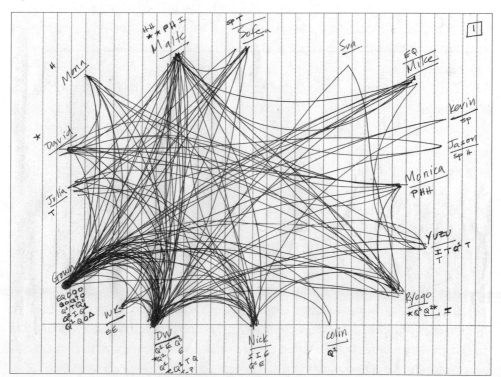

acknowledged several of the same aspects I had noticed. We agreed to tackle them on day 2.

Despite our debriefing session, the second day produced the same results. Gown asked even more questions than the previous day and the shy kids spoke as little as or less than the first day.

I then decided to employ a technique I have had to use over the years a handful of times with a few superstars, which is to ask them to spend an entire discussion silent, only observing and taking notes. I once watched a student squirm and squeal from her seat for 40 minutes because she wanted to share in the exchange of ideas and she was so disturbed that she couldn't. "Can't I just say one thing?" she begged periodically, and I would shake my head, no. I do this to help those superstars experience another kind of class discussion and a potential new role for them in it. For one, it's good to be forced to listen sometimes, especially for those of us who love to hear ourselves talk. Secondly, as with team players on the sideline of a game, it's often much easier to see the big picture when not in the middle of the playing field. Those students who have had to spend a discussion or two in silence have often reported a heightened awareness of the group dynamic and how the discussion measures up against the rubric criteria.

On the third day, I asked Gown to do just this, to remain silent during the discussion.

"But I'm only trying to help everyone else talk! I'm worried about the grade!" she pleaded. I understood her argument perfectly, but I encouraged her to give it a try for one day. In my experience, when a superstar is silent, space opens up for several more moderate or reticent talkers to engage. It tends to have a balancing effect that students notice and can acknowledge in the day's debriefing process.

Figure 4.2 shows the web graph of that day 3 discussion, in which Gown was asked not to speak at all.

You might have noticed that Gown still spoke. Three times. She was so hard-wired to speak, to be a superstar (and to be rewarded for that), that she couldn't help herself and continued to participate, forgetting that she wasn't supposed to. Each time she would clap her hand over her mouth and apologize in earnest. She was so conditioned to speak that she had a very hard time not speaking.

Figure 4.2 **E Block Gown Still Speaks**

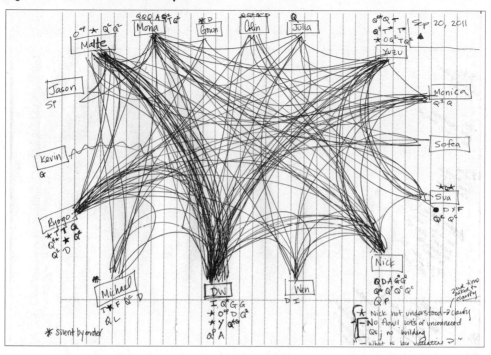

Eventually, over the weeks and months that followed, our Spider Web Discussion work began to pay off. Figures 4.3 and 4.4 show web graphs from February and March of that same school year (about six months after the first discussion).

One thing you can see right away is that the webs themselves are "prettier"; they look more like real spider webs. That's because students are pulling their own weight much more, contributing more evenly, and so there is far more balance to the web. Like a real spider web, our webs need to be balanced and each person or anchor point needs to pull his or her own weight evenly or the web will collapse. In these later discussions, Gown participates less than Sua, one of the shyest students in the class. We find that students like Sua are not so shy when allowed more space, and there is a greater sense of balance as the class benefits from more voices.

Figure 4.3 **E Block More Balanced Discussion**

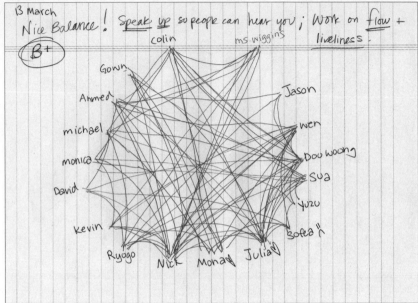

Figure 4.4 **E Block First A–**

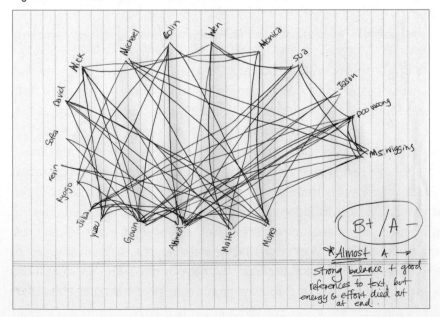

Paradoxically, more voices means fewer contributions. You can also see in the later discussions that the volume of contributions in general has diminished significantly. At first you might think this is undesirable, but fewer contributions mean longer, more thoughtful responses. It means more listening and less disconnected chatter or questioning. It shows quality over quantity. After six months of weekly discussions and debriefings, the students had finally begun to meet the criteria, and the discussions were richer for it. It was wonderful to hear students like Sua, Julia, and Ryogo shine where before Doo Wong and Gown had dominated. The shy kids and the superstars had learned to meet in the middle.

Sometimes the opposite problem occurs: a class is not too reticent but too enthusiastic. The same year I was teaching the taciturn E block class, I taught the boisterous B block class. In this class, there was hardly a reticent student. From the very first day, the students in B block were like overenthusiastic puppies jumping over one another to try to play with the ball. It seemed everyone wanted to speak, nobody wanted to listen, and everyone interrupted constantly. The overabundance of energy and enthusiasm was easier to deal with than the shyness and silence of E block, but it still needed to be dealt with. Figure 4.5 shows the graph of B block's first Spider Web Discussion.

You can see that not only was there an abundance of participation by a majority of students, there was also a significant imbalance in this class. Several students spoke little and one student, Caleb, didn't speak at all.

During the first debriefing, they laughed when I shared the graph with them and they saw how many times they had interrupted each other. To this day, I have never seen a discussion with so many interruptions. I asked the students what needed to happen to improve the next discussion, and they offered suggestions: taking turns, speaking less, helping others get into the conversation.

The B block class was very excited and enthusiastic about the SWD process. At the next class period, several students bounded in, sat at the desks, and asked, "Can we do that discussion thing again?" They seemed giddy at the prospect of having ownership and voice during class time. In this particular group of students—mostly boys—the method had struck a chord. They felt completely switched on, something I was thrilled by, given recent news reports about performance and engagement of boys in school.

Figure 4.5 **B Block First Day Boisterousness**

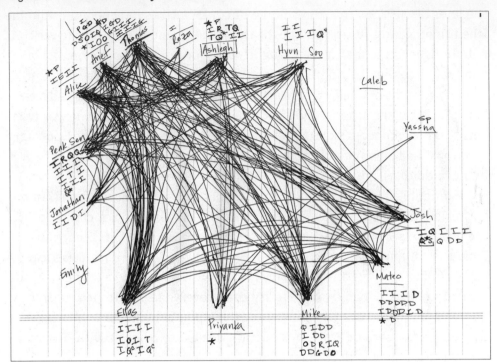

The second day wasn't terribly different, however, as you'll see in Figure 4.6. The interruptions were just as bad. The same students that dominated the first day also dominated the second day, and the same students who had held back, still held back. Just like E block, the students were not yet learning from the feedback. The two classes were discussing the same texts at the same time and having two very different Spider Web Discussion experiences. As every teacher knows, this is not unusual. You can present the same content in the same way to two different classes and have two vastly different experiences. It's one reason why the rubric and the norming process for Spider Web Discussion are so powerful; over years of teaching this way, I have seen a 100 percent success rate in moving students from chaotic, imbalanced, scattered, debate-like discussions to more balanced, deeper conversations. Despite real challenges with certain groups or individual students, by bringing students back to the criteria each

Figure 4.6 **B Block Still Too Many Interruptions on Day Two**

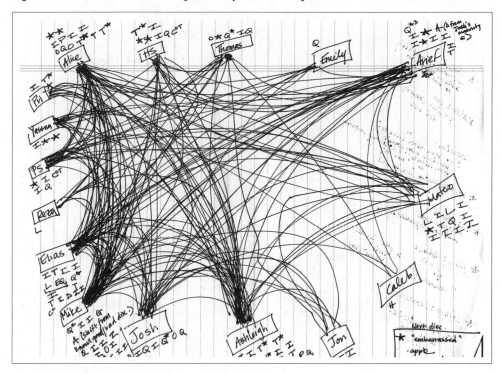

time and asking them to assess their own collective performance, I see results. Every single class has improved. (See Figure 4.6.)

B block took almost as much time to get there as E block. We had to work on harnessing their tremendous enthusiasm as a "force for good" instead of for evil. This meant debriefs during which we openly discussed the problems with interruptions, imbalance, and unfocused inquiry.

By the end of that same month, the graph looked different (see Figure 4.7). What do you notice in comparison to the first two? The interruptions have decreased greatly, which was one of our goals. But so has the volume of comments—there are fewer lines being drawn in general, which evinces more listening and less frenetic responding.

By February, the class had self-assigned their first *A* (see Figure 4.8).

There are only two interruptions noted during the entire discussion, and the volume and balance are close to optimal. When we all agreed together on

Figure 4.7 **B Block Improvement After One Month**

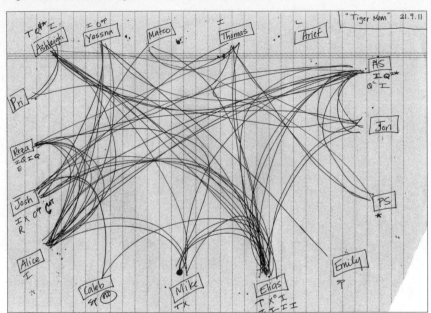

Figure 4.8 **B Block February First *A*–**

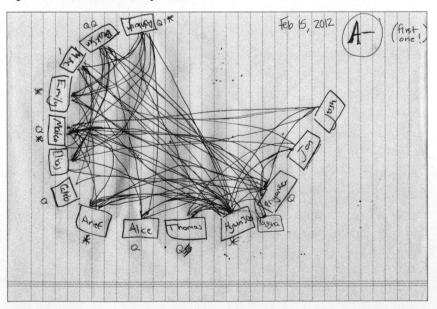

the *A*- as the best fit for the day's discussions, there were loud cheers and clapping. This is one of the things I love about Spider Web Discussion: it rewards patience, persistence, and a reliance on self-assessing against clear criteria. Students aren't left wondering when the teacher will "ever" give them an *A*, or questioning why they got the grade they did. Instead, they are deeply involved in a process, working toward the goal of an *A*, a process that rewards autonomy, strong leadership and social skills, and a focus on clear criteria.

In March, the class achieved its top grade of the year (see Figure 4.9). Although Mike and a few other students participate more than Caleb, four comments during one discussion is significant growth for Caleb when you compare the class's early discussions. And Mike is no longer interrupting and is listening a lot more. There is far less disparity in the amount of contributions made by the middle of the year.

Figure 4.9 **B Block March Best Discussion of the Year**

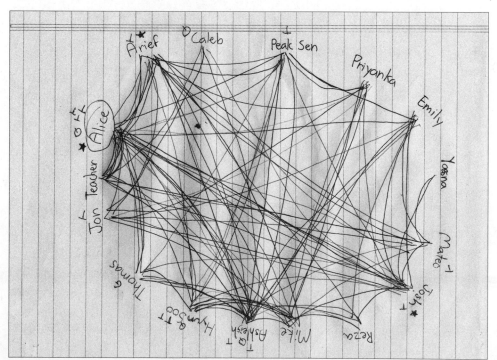

I've realized over the years that the best discussions always look more beautiful on paper. Just like a spider web in nature, the graph from Spider Web Discussions reflects that beauty of a balanced conversation based on listening and quality contribution.

We reach this level of beauty by coaching our students, especially the shy kids and the superstars, to see the bigger picture—the teamwork—and not just their individual role.

What the Research Says

In the beginning, I worried more about superstars and shy kids feeling punished by this kind of method. I questioned whether it was fair to ask students to step out of their comfort zones. Wasn't I just going against the grain of who these kids truly were? Was it fair to ask the Gowns to be more quiet and ask the Calebs to speak up? In both her book, *Quiet*, and her TED Talk, Susan Cain discusses the tendency in school systems to value group work and collaboration over individual work and quiet time, a process that she sees as rewarding extroverts and hindering introverts. In a 2016 article published in *New York Magazine's Science of Us* site, Melissa Dahl interviews Susan Cain about her Quiet Schools Network and the research on introverts. It turns out there is some evidence that introverts may have different physiological responses to stimulation. Specifically, extroverts naturally have a low level of arousal in certain areas of the brain, while introverts have high levels of arousal in those areas. Because successful performance of tasks requires a medium level of arousal, extroverts are generally trying to increase their level of arousal while introverts are trying to decrease theirs (Dahl, 2106). The Quiet Schools Network encourages teachers to think about classroom engagement rather than classroom participation to recognize that there are other ways to measure students' understanding of the material than "how quickly and loudly they can talk about it" (Dahl, 2016).

It's true that schools tend to value collaboration and extroversion over independent quiet time for students, and I think more could be done to allow for reflective, individual-based problem solving and reflection in K–16 education. But I find this article relevant to the aims of Spider Web Discussion because it highlights the assumption that the only alternative to introversion is superstar behavior. By saying that there might be other ways to measure understanding than "how quickly and loudly they can talk about it" assumes a false dichotomy that we either have quiet reflection or quick and loud participation. In this chapter, you can see that quick and loud participation doesn't lead to great discussions or strong collaboration. When the scales are tipped too far toward the "yang" behavior of superstars, as in the example of my B block class, the discussion never takes flight. But when the scales are tipped too far toward the "yin" behavior of introverts or shy students, the result is equally unproductive. There is a place for both extroverts and introverts in Spider Web Discussion. By creating very clear norms that value listening over quickness and balance over loudness, we signal to the group that inquiry and teamwork is the bigger picture. By allowing students to give endless opinions, interrupt, and monopolize the talk time, we are teaching the wrong lesson about what productive shared inquiry—not to mention civility—should look like. But the answer is not, as Cain assures us, to swing to the other extreme in favor of introvert-only models. She and her Quiet Schools Movement head, Heidi Kasevich, make the case for a more balanced approach to learning, one that helps quiet students be more comfortable with talking in class. "None of this, incidentally, is about excluding the loud kids, who will still be able to talk through their thoughts. It's about helping the quiet kids recognize that their thoughts are worth sharing, too" (Dahl, 2016).

My only concern with that point is that the "loud kids will still be able to talk through their thoughts." I'd argue that as educators we are not doing our jobs well if we don't also teach the *loud* kids that the quiet kids' thoughts are indeed worth sharing, and that they need to be less loud to allow us to hear the quiet kids.

You can see it when you see a strong, mid-year Spider Web Discussion: the graph of the web looks beautiful, there is balance, less volume, more listening, less chaos or dead air. The goal for all types of students—shy kids, superstars, and everyone in between —is balanced, productive discussion. By challenging introverts and extroverts to come outside their comfort zones, we all benefit.

Practical Considerations

How do you get superstars and shy kids to come outside their comfort zones? Through feedback.

In the early months, you will constantly be helping students assess their work as a group and as individuals through the rubric, the coding, and the debriefing. A student like Vanessa from the opening vignette is naturally going to be uncomfortable that she is no longer rewarded for her endless, insightful contributions during class time, and she will quite possibly be confused or even angry that the rules of the game she has learned to play so well have suddenly changed. It's important, then, to be kind to the students who struggle with this shift and help them see that their contributions can be even more valuable than ever in this new model. I have taught many students like Vanessa and Gown who were used to getting more praise and better grades the more they spoke up. But because this was the role they had settled into, few of them had ever been challenged to push their boundaries and skills further. For example, Gown had never been asked to be quiet before. She didn't have a context for understanding what that experience could be like, and she found it almost impossible to do. This was important feedback for her, and the lessons she learned (about listening, observing, and how "loud" she was in discussions) by having to adopt a silent observer role twice in class helped shape her into a more mature thinker and collaborator.

Another student of mine, Omnia, a superstar who was one of the brightest students I had ever taught, was not used to being asked to be quiet, either; she laughed and made faces of mock pain throughout the discussion when she wasn't allowed to speak. Omnia learned something from these limitations—that perhaps where there is pain and discomfort, there also lies a valuable lesson. In this case, how much do I really need to talk in order to benefit the group? Do I need to respond to everything that is said? How could the discussion benefit from me in ways I haven't yet considered?

With especially bright students like Vanessa or Omnia, I find the answer is to teach them how to ask great questions. In order to ask great questions, you need to be an astute listener and be able to detect the bigger picture—the themes that tie the conversation together. I try to model this myself during a discussion that is putting along just fine but not getting very deep or productive. I will usually throw out a provocative idea that sparks a lot of interest and back and forth. For example, if the students are discussing *Romeo and Juliet* and are spinning their wheels a bit about fate and the role of family, I might ask, "Do parents always know what's best for their children?" and follow it up with, "Do your parents know what's best for you?" A question or two like this is bound to spark a strong reaction and engagement from young adolescents, and it usually sets the conversation in another direction about fate, family, and the right to personal happiness. Later, during the debrief, I would ask, "What happened when I asked that question about parents? Did you see how it set you guys off and running in a whole other direction that led to deeper exploration and understanding of the text? That's what I want you guys to get good at doing. Noticing what big picture isn't being seen, what question isn't being asked, what understanding and connections have not yet been grasped." I might sit down with Omnia or Vanessa alone and explain that I understand why she is struggling because I, too, struggle when I have to listen more than I talk. I try to get her to understand that an adult leader is often the one who poses a good, well-placed question—worth more than 100 opinions—and that I am relying on her to lead by example.

With shy kids, I have evolved in my thinking about how best to support them in Spider Web Discussion thanks to a student of mine named Ali. Before I taught Ali, I had always assumed that shy kids had little or nothing to contribute. I couldn't imagine that people who had something they really wanted to contribute would sit there silently.

It was a surprise, then, when I interviewed and recorded my 11th grade IB English class in 2010 about their experience with Spider Web Discussion. I had several superstars—including Omnia—in that class, and one terribly shy student, Ali. Ali had rarely spoken during the year, save for a lone comment or two each day. He was an average student in my class who struggled with deeper concepts, but he was always alert, eager, on task, and seemed to prefer listening to speaking. The first question I had planned to ask him on film was this one: *Would you consider yourself a talkative person or a shy person in class discussion?* I wanted to highlight his shy nature as part of the video I was making because I thought it was important to hear from students who had varied personalities and experiences using the method. I assumed he would talk about how it was hard for him to do Spider Web Discussion because he was shy but that it ultimately allowed him a chance to express himself from time to time, which was what I had observed.

His reply caught me by surprise. He responded, "I would consider myself a shy person, except I think I would consider myself to have a lot of things to say." I had taught him for a year and if you had asked me to wager, I would never have bet that Ali saw himself as someone who had "a lot of things to say." I had always assumed his reticence meant he had little to say. Here is the transcript of the rest of our brief interview:

Alexis: *Do you normally get to say those things in regular class discussions (in other classes)?*

Ali: (hesitant, thinking) *No.*

Alexis: *Why not?*

Ali: (Laughs) *Uh, I think I like to see what other people say and just use their ideas instead of my own.*

Alexis: *And do the teachers usually call on you?*

Ali: *In regular discussions?*

Alexis: *Yes.*

Ali: *Uh, no.*

Alexis: *Why not?*

Ali: *I don't raise my hand. (Laughs)*

Ali was a student who identified as shy, but as having a lot to say, who spoke up occasionally in our class only because the criteria required it, and in traditional settings he chose to use other people's ideas instead of his own or not participate at all. I thought of Ali often as I forged ahead with Spider Web Discussion. His conviction when he assertively describes himself as someone who "has a lot to say" showed me that Spider Web Discussion isn't about forcing students to be who they aren't; it's allowing them to be who they really are. Ali saw himself as someone with a lot to contribute, and in his mind, he *was* contributing a lot with his comment or two a day. It was double the amount of participation he was engaging in compared to other classes, and the reason that he was able to do that is because the superstars in the class were being asked to listen and question more, and he was being encouraged to speak up. There was space for Ali to be a contributor, and he was rewarded for unique ideas, not just regurgitating his peers' or teacher's thoughts.

I am still in touch with Ali and he has grown into a thoughtful, funny, and quick-witted young man in his 20s. In fact, you can read his testimonial at the end of this chapter. I'm glad I was his teacher, but I'm also grateful that he got to be mine. Ali taught me that my assumptions about quiet, shy people were far off base. Quiet people do have lots to say—they just need the space and the safety in which to say it. Remember the key findings of Google's Project Aristotle, cited in Chapter 2: the most productive teams have norms that promote equal talk time and a feeling of safety.

Supporting shy kids and superstars through navigating outside their comfort zones is important. As a teacher, you need to work hard to make Spider Web Discussions respectful, fruitful, and safe for all kinds of students and learners. When students put a shy kid on the spot and he can't handle the pressure and mumbles an "I don't know" until the awkward silence passes and the discussion moves on, I always address this in the debrief. I will ask how that went, I will ask students how it feels to be put on the spot, and most admit it doesn't feel good. I will then ask if there are other, better strategies for including someone into the conversation. I might suggest that a shy kid begin the discussion with a quote or a question, as that often feels easier than offering one's own opinion or waiting for a quiet moment in which to jump in, something shy kids regularly cite as the reason they didn't get to contribute. This way, we slowly build safety and community within the framework—we are all in this together, and the students can learn some key leadership qualities, such as that putting someone on the spot isn't the best strategy for collaborative inquiry.

As a nod to Susan Cain's work and to support any introverts in your class, you might ask all students to take a moment before the discussion for some quiet reflection. They could write down their answers to a particular essential question about the text or topic about to be discussed, individually and in silence, before the collaborative portion. This practice provides the introverts some time to process their ideas and reflect on them in a way that best suits them before having to push outside their comfort zone.

Advanced Applications

It isn't only introverts who benefit from writing or sketching ideas before discussion. One way to help all students, especially introverts, learning disabled, and English language learners, is to use Dialectical Journals, or "DJs," as I like to call them, to help students think critically about the text before they discuss it.

The way I use DJs in the classroom is to ask students to create a page and divide it in half vertically. In the left column they copy a quote of their choosing from the text. In the right column they analyze the quote in a brief paragraph. I've included some examples from my high school English students' DJs. Figure 4.10 is from a 9th grade student. The text they were reading was *Flowers for Algernon*.

As you can see, this student is having a personal dialogue with the text, interacting with it and reacting to it in her DJ entry. Students can write in paragraph form, bullet point, or through drawings and diagrams—or a combination of all of them—as they grapple with the critical thinking and application of their analytical skills.

Here is an example from a 12th grade student's Dialectical Journal on *Things Fall Apart*:

	Quote	Notes	Themes
1.	"And when she returned he beat her very heavily. In his anger he had forgotten that it was the Week of Peace" P23–24	• Violent nature of Okonkwo ("whenever he was angry and . . . he would use his fists" P3) • Obedience and inferiority of the wives • Foreshadowing of an event, or something that might happen to Okonkwo–breaking with the gods (during the Week of Peace, one is not supposed to be violent) • Will there be any reaction from the wives' side?	Violence Men vs women Religion Justice

You'll notice that this student began a third column, "Themes," to track the literary themes she found as she read the novel.

Figure 4.10 **Example of High School English Student's DJ**

Quotation and page #	Analysis
1. "Then Miss Kinnian came to see me and she brout me some magizenes to read, and she lookd kind of nervus and skared" (9)	- We can see Miss Kinian cares about Charlie because she brings him something to read. - She also shows concern for him because she is described as "nervus" and "skared." I think she might be nervous for him because she is the one that recommended the operation so she is maybe feeling some guilt in case it doesn't go well. - Charlie still cannot spell very well. His spelling seems like a child's. - However, I noticed that he used a comma for the first time in his writing. This could be an example of how he is growing and learning already even if he isn't aware of it yet.

Figure 4.11 shows the Dialectical Journal of an 11th grade IB student. She built on the theme's idea by using coding to enhance her DJ on the Greek tragedy *Oedipus the King*.

Figure 4.12 is a journal example from a 12th grade IB literature class. The format is slightly different and more prescribed, based on the Jane Schaffer paragraph method, a method that helps students organize their ideas in analytical/literary essays. You can see the instructions for how to do the DJ entry in the first row.

Allowing students to bring in journal entries or texts with notes so that they can draw upon their reflections during the discussions has been successful.

Figure 4.11 **Oedipus Entry**

Quote	Response	Main Lit. Features
1) Priest: "Now we **pray** to you. **You cannot equal the gods**, you children know that, bending at your **altar**. But we do rate you first of men, both in the common crises of our lives and face-to-face encounters with the **gods**. You freed us from the Sphinx, you came to Thebes and cut us loose from the bloody tribute we had paid that harsh, brutal singer. We taught you nothing, no skill, no extra knowledge, still you triumphed. **A god was with you**, so they say, and we believe it—you lifted up our lives" (161)	• Citizens: Oedipus' "children." This means that they have a good close connection. • **Bending at your altar** is a sign of respect. They respect their king Oedipus. • They praise their king, but the **gods are at a whole other level**. There is no comparison between a human and the gods: **Strong faith**. • Believe that a god was with him in everything he did for Thebes, which again shows the power of the gods and their importance. • **The priest speaks for all of them**: they viewed the gods and all that is linked with the gods to be very important and reliable. • Praising diction: "you triumphed" and "rate you first of men." • Formal diction: shows importance of king. • Long formal syntax/style: importance of king.	Characterization of Oedipus Themes/main ideas: **Faith**, **importance of the gods**

Key:

Characterization (underline)

Faith (bold)

Importance of gods (gray highlight)

Hubris (italics)

Humans have flaws (dark gray highlight)

Attempting to escape fate (black highlight)

Foreshadowing (gray text)

IRONY (ALL CAPS)

Source: Used with permission from Maha Al Ansari.

Figure 4.12 **Dialectical Journal Entry on Hamlet**

Source Material (Provide a direct quotation or paraphrase and a parenthetical citation) (CD)	RESPOND (This is your initial reaction or response—what does the quote make you think/feel/remember/want to know?) **ANALYZE** (What techniques are the author using, and how do they affect the reader? It may be only one technique.) (CM1), and **EVALUATE** (How effective was the author using this/these technique/s and how did it/they affect the story?) (CM2) **DJ entry Word Count**	Theme
"O that this too too solid flesh would melt/ Thaw, and resolve itself into a dew!/ Or that the Everlasting had not fix'd/ His canon 'gainst self-slaughter! O God! O God!/ How weary, stale, flat, and unprofitable/ Seem to me all the uses of this world!" (I.ii.131–61) Hamlet to Rosencrantz	**RESPOND:** Hamlet speaking here. Poor Hamlet. He's so low that he contemplates suicide. This reminds me of the two guys I know from the past three years that killed themselves. Why is suicide more likely in men than in women? I feel Hamlet's teenage angst here deeply. I often feel like the world doesn't make sense and my parents only make things worse not better—so I empathize with him in this passage. **ANALYZE:** Hamlet emphasizes his angst here through repetition and the theme of **doubt.** Hamlet wishes he could commit suicide but what stops him? The threat of permanent purgatory/punishment for the sin of suicide—"the Everlasting." This introduces the dual idea of good/evil and life/death (suicide). Shakespeare uses vivid imagery and diction—"flesh" "melting" and "thawing" to describe his emotions. These are all words related to temperature—hot and cold. Normally they would describe objects, like ice or a cadaver. **EVALUATE:** Hamlet comes across as a little dramatic—are we meant to see him as overdramatic? Or are we meant to empathize with him? The vivid imagery and diction—melting flesh—almost repels or disgusts the reader. It's gross to imagine flesh "melting" or rotting (connection to theme of decay/rottenness!), as if our bodies were only objects and not really living things. Is Shakespeare suggesting that suicide is revolting? Or that life is revolting? I think Hamlet comes across as sympathetic here and that, ultimately, Shakespeare aims for that, because he is using the repetition of "O God! O God" to show that Hamlet is having a crisis of conscience—life has become so unbearable and depressing that he would prefer not to live it, but he cannot end it because he will go to hell. Is that not a kind of hell itself? Is Shakespeare suggesting as much—that life itself is hell? It certainly seems to be so in Hamlet's circumstances—his father dead, murdered, his uncle married to his mother, and the family plotting behind his back. Hamlet—impotent and (acting) mad.	• Doubt • Life/Death (suicide) • Rotte/diseased body

It leads to much better textual citations and support than using the original text alone. It also provides introverts, or students who struggle with analysis or speaking the target language, with a sense of safety, something tangible in front of them that they can rely on to help frame their contribution or support their idea. Additionally, if you focus your grading and reporting on the journals and the individual thinking and growth demonstrated in each student's journal over the course of the year, there is little pushback on using a no-count group grade for the discussions because there is ample evidence of individual students' ability and progress. For any teacher anxious about introducing the group grade, I strongly recommend using dialectical journals. They can be adapted to almost any course's aims by asking students to think critically and problem solve or analyze course content. Using Dialectical Journals daily or weekly will provide more than enough grades in the grade book to accurately reflect the individual student's understanding and synthesis of course material. In this way, group grades for the discussion itself will be accurate feedback on the *group's* progress, complementing the "counted" grading and reporting on *individual students'* progress from the Dialectical Journals.

I have found that allowing students to use their DJs on laptops or tablets during class time is not productive. In every class, at all age levels, I have always observed a core group of students easily distracted by social media, sports sites, or messaging apps as they try to engage in discussion. It's impossible to monitor all screens at once. I have had students request to have "no laptops" included in the norms because they themselves realized that screens prevented the discussions from reaching their full potential. Over the years, the best system I have come up with involves asking students to bring in their handwritten journal or a printout of the previous night's journal entry. I firmly believe that students' screens, though an excellent invention and a great boon during many class activities, do not have a place during Spider Web Discussion.

Using Dialectical Journals, or just asking students to jot down their key points or questions before discussion, can provide needed reflection time for all students, especially introverts and those with specific learning needs. Dialectical Journals also provide another way, in addition to Spider Web Discussion, for you to observe students' critical thinking and communication skills before a high-stakes assessment.

Voices from the Field

—ALI AL-ANI, ENGINEERING STUDENT, AMERICAN UNIVERSITY OF SHARJAH (SHARJAH, U.A.E.)—Being the quiet student that I was, Spider Web Discussion was an uncomfortable idea for me. I was expected to share my thoughts and opinions unprompted, and this was the biggest challenge for me. Often times I found myself thinking "Yeah, exactly" throughout the discussions, but I wouldn't add to the conversation. It also didn't help that a few of the other students would take every opportunity to speak up, often controlling the direction the discussion would go in, and perhaps leaving me behind thinking about the previous topic. Spider Web Discussion was a new format for the whole class, so for a while we were being very experimental with it. The discussion would often start its focus on a piece of literature but would then evolve into a philosophical exchange.

It wasn't until I felt that the other students were affected by my input that I became more involved with the discussions. I wasn't directly asked for my opinion, but I also grew tired of just having my thoughts float around in my head. I grew less interested in having people agree with me and more excited to ask a thought-provoking question or raise an idea that would force the class to pause for a second. It became an opportunity to intellectually explore in a way that I wasn't used to, and I fell in love with it very quickly. It forced me to think not only about the others' thoughts, but also about my own.

Big Takeaway

The superstars and the shy kids have their place in the world, but we aren't doing our students any favors by rewarding them for behavior that runs counter to productive collaboration. The greatest learning opportunities for students come when we challenge them in just the right ways, pushing them a bit outside their comfort zones so they can experience a new way of thinking or working.

Think back to one of the times you learned a key concept or important lesson in your education. I'm willing to bet that it was an incident that pushed you into new, shaky territory. I recall when I was struggling mightily in a college physics course despite a great deal of time and effort. I arranged to meet with the professor weekly in the mornings before class leading up to the exam because my GPA and an important scholarship were resting on my getting a *B* or better for the course. Despite my best efforts, I had a *C+* average. The morning sessions were helping, but I still struggled with a course that I would never have taken if my university didn't require it. I recall feeling annoyed that I had to take a course that I didn't like, didn't believe I would need in the future, and was hard for me. I vividly remember the weekend before the final exam sitting down to study the material one last time, but this time I approached it from an entirely different angle. Suddenly something clicked. I "saw" the physics in a new, visual way and it made sense and seemed simpler than I had seen it before. I aced the exam, just managing a *B* for the overall course, and was able to keep my scholarship. I felt incredibly proud. It was pretty easy for me to feel confident in the courses for my English major and Spanish minor, but I don't remember those learning experiences as vividly because I wasn't challenged by them in the same way. We learn the most when we are challenged. Spider Web Discussion involves challenging students to overcome discomfort, whether that is through speaking up, staying quiet, or owning their inquiry.

5 ROADBLOCKS LATER ON: THAT ONE TOUGH CLASS

Rob was a 7th grade social studies teacher who had attended some professional development on Spider Web Discussion and was eager to give it a try in his classroom. Using the guidelines he had learned, he developed a rubric and a few lessons. The first discussion was far better than he had anticipated, and he relaxed, realizing there was a place for the method in his classroom. During those first weeks, the level of enthusiasm was higher than normal as students took charge of their own learning and questioning. But after the second or third discussion, Rob noticed one boy, Adam, who wasn't speaking up during the discussions. Rob openly addressed this as gently as possible during the first debrief, but Adam didn't appear fazed. He crossed his arms and said, "I don't feel like talking." Adam was known to be stubborn and got into disciplinary trouble from time to time at school, but so far in Rob's class, he hadn't created much of an issue. Until now.

During the next couple weeks, despite the rest of the class soaring with Spider Web Discussion, Adam refused to budge. He almost seemed to enjoy the role of dissenter, relishing in his peers' and his teacher's frustration at his refusal to follow the criteria (thereby bringing down the group grade). Adam was absent one day and the SWD was the best it had ever been—the students and Rob decided together that it was their first *A*. But Adam would be back in school the following week, and then what? Rob needed a strategy to deal with this boy who had dug in his heels and seemed to enjoy the power he had to bring down the discussion.

Each class has its own dynamic, its own characters, and its own particular chemistry. As a teacher, I have to adapt to them each year. I have never had two classes approach Spider Web Discussion the same way and I enjoy the challenge of figuring out how to problem solve a new group's unique challenges.

One situation a few years ago nearly made me throw in the towel. Thanks to one supersonic star in my class, I didn't know if I could navigate the waters with that class and not smash the ship against the rocks.

Jack was a high school junior who monopolized all discussions, loved to shout down everyone else, and relished saying things to provoke his classmates or me (e.g., "women are whiny"). Early in the year, Jack's mom scheduled a meeting with me to make sure I understood his unique qualities, one of which was challenging his teachers. She explained that Jack hadn't liked one of his freshman teachers and didn't believe she was a good teacher because she didn't teach grammar. In a clash of personalities, Jack and this teacher had battled all year. The battle involved many meetings with parents and administrators, and Jack's mother felt that a lot of negativity could have been avoided with a different approach. I was grateful for these preemptive insights and vowed to "kill 'em with kindness," as my mother always advised.

From the first weeks, I understood the challenge. Jack loved to hear himself talk. Jack stymied discussion by responding to every single student's observation throughout every discussion. The pattern of our discussions was such that one student spoke, and Jack responded. Another student spoke, Jack responded again. A third student spoke, and Jack responded to her. Jack began every response with, "I agree," or "I disagree." I realized within a few classes that Jack believed discussion in English class was an exercise in saying whether he agreed with any voiced opinion. I tried a variety of tactics. I talked at length during debriefings about the importance of having a balanced discussion and not letting one person dominate. This subtle message was lost on Jack, who continued to believe the discussion was all about him.

After a week or so of this kind of fruitless feedback, I happened to be talking with Jack about a separate issue. I took advantage of the occasion to encourage him to be more of a leader in discussion, to use his talent and intellect to help raise the level of conversation by asking interesting questions rather than spouting an opinion. During the next class discussion, Jack did ask a couple of interesting questions, but as soon as one student gave a brief or superficial answer, Jack swooped in with his own insights, unable to let the conversation develop without him at the center.

Jack was trying my patience and my repertoire of strategies, as well as affecting the class morale. I could see on the other students' faces that they were uncomfortable with and annoyed by Jack's behavior, but they were resigned to it. This worried me because, as a teacher, I believe one of my biggest jobs is to make the environment safe and welcoming.

I went back to the drawing board. How could I get Jack to listen—really listen—to his peers and allow them the space to communicate in a way that didn't seem like a punishment to him? That's when I hit on it: roles.

I designed a series of roles for the whole-group discussion that asked different students to accomplish different tasks. One role was to be the "feedback giver," a student who doesn't participate at all by speaking, but takes copious notes on the discussion—what went well and what could have been stronger, given our rubric. The first time I assigned Jack this role, he stayed silent the whole class, then gave very critical feedback on all the ideas the students didn't discuss—or discuss well enough—according to him. Another role was "three-question asker." The student in this role could speak only three times during the whole conversation, with each contribution being the best discussion-inspiring question he could think of. Once Jack had asked his three questions, though, he tuned out completely. He began to do homework for another class. It was still all about Jack.

Yet another role was "host." This role asked students to be aware of any peers who weren't actively involved in the discussion and to invite them into the fold. The day that Jack was asked to be host, he was responding to a girl's comment (for the umpteenth time) with, "I agree, but . . ." and I saw him catch himself and remember that he was supposed to play host. Not playing the role adequately could affect the class discussion grade and Jack cared a lot about grades.

Jack awkwardly turned to a bright but shy student and asked, "What do you think, Marcus? What did you find in last night's reading?" Marcus didn't skip a beat in sharing what he'd noticed in Tobias Wolff's *In Pharaoh's Army*.

"There's this motif related to time, especially to watches," Marcus said. He went on to cite three quotes about watches from the reading, providing a nuanced and insightful look at the relationship between time and death in the text. I was impressed. I had taught the book twice before and had never noticed the motif. Jack was also impressed and nodded enthusiastically. He hadn't noticed the watch motif either, but it made perfect sense to him, and he seemed excited by it. "I agree," he enthused while underlining the passages.

During the debriefing of this discussion, I focused on that moment and showed how Jack had tossed the ball to Marcus and we'd all benefited. It perfectly illustrated the erroneous thinking that shy people have nothing to say and that the loudest kids are the smart ones with all the right answers. This was a turning point for the discussions in general. I think it might have been the first time that Jack realized he could actually benefit from others in the room, especially from someone more reticent. For the few months that remained in the school year, Jack was noticeably less "alpha" during discussions. His aggressive approach to responding to everyone abated. He was still an active participant and loved to challenge others and disagree with their positions, but the edge was gone. There was far less bluster and arrogance in the way he spoke. Marcus's insight into the watch motif had intellectually excited Jack. When he finally realized that it had taken his own silence to allow that important textual detail to emerge, there was a subtle but real shift in his behavior. I think we all breathed a little sigh of relief then, feeling that our class discussions became more of a shared inquiry and less of a debate against Jack.

I tell the story of Jack to introduce you to the roles that I developed that might help you make the most out of Spider Web Discussion in your classroom, but also to elucidate three important points: First, I want to remind you again that this is a process, much like writing or reading. If you think of it as a one-time approach or something you can ask students to do from time to time, then it won't be much different from any other discussion approach you may try. But if you understand and embrace the process approach to Spider Web Discussion, then you begin to see it as an opportunity to push your students beyond what they think is possible and to do the same for yourself. I was near tears for weeks with Jack, thinking he was the student who "broke" Spider Web Discussion for me after five years of success. It took me many tries at troubleshooting, talking with colleagues and mentors, and failed attempts until I hit upon the use of roles and had a breakthrough. This point is not meant to weigh you down with the concept that Spider Web Discussion is something complicated or burdensome. I certainly never found it that way. It is simply a reminder that if it doesn't go swimmingly all the time (and it won't), just remember that it's like teaching writing or critical thinking—we don't introduce it and leave it alone for the students to figure out. We take years helping students grasp and practice these abilities, and we often have to adapt our teaching or lesson plans based on their needs, triumphs, and trials with those skills.

Second, I tell you the story of Jack to highlight a related but slightly different point, which is that the best growth I have had as a teacher is through Spider Web Discussion because it is almost never the same thing twice. I never get bored in classes because each day we create something almost entirely different. When it began to feel stale or repetitive, I would strategize and try something new, like introducing a provocative reading that I knew would spark debate. Jack and Gown pushed me out of my comfort zone. It's much easier to have a class that fluidly runs itself with a group of high performers that all behave ethically, contribute equally, and prepare fully for discussions, but this is rare. I confess I find those classes a little boring. When deep in the experience with Jack, I certainly wasn't enjoying it. I was really struggling with my teaching, my method, and my class. But within a few months' time, I was grateful for him and the lessons he taught me, because it pushed me to develop new ways of teaching and thinking, and I think the whole class benefited. In short, Spider Web Discussion not only gives students the chance to think and collaborate in ways they haven't been asked to (or rewarded for) before, it also gives *you* the same opportunity. Embrace it, and don't worry about the hurdles. They are just temporary. Take the long view and set your sights on what kind of classroom-based discussion you'd like to see by the end of the year. Design backward from that and any problems that develop on the way should be seen as opportunities.

Third, I want to stress that empathy in the classroom is hard work. There were days when I wished Jack would switch to a colleague's section so I'd be rid of him. I even cried on a particularly frustrating day because not only did his behavior irritate me, it also made me feel guilty that I was letting the rest of the class down. The other students weren't benefitting from the method because Jack was dominating every moment. It would have been easier to give up and switch back to a teacher-centered mode of inquiry, a more traditional

Socratic approach in which I directed the conversation and called on specific people. This would have allowed me to "manage" Jack more easily and protect the other students from his commandeering every discussion. But we would have missed some key opportunities, not the least of which is the chance to experience empathy and compassion for one another. Jack needed to learn that Marcus (and others) had excellent contributions to make. Until the day when Marcus spoke about the watch motif, Jack acted as if he were the only person in the class with anything intelligent to offer. It made it hard to empathize with him, and it made it impossible for him to feel empathy for his classmates. If I had stepped in and abandoned the principals of Spider Web Discussion—the student-driven, collaborative approach—we all would have missed a chance to grow. As we struggled through the term together, I watched as we slowly began to feel more like a team. The energy in the room changed. In the first weeks, students had come in and sat in little cliques, mostly keeping to themselves when not in discussion mode and rarely interacting with each other. There hadn't been much laughter or sharing in those first weeks, and there had been little intellectual or emotional risk-taking during discussion.

The whole dynamic shifted when we began to struggle through the process together, building our team through trial and error. By the spring term, there was a palpable loosening of tension. Students who hadn't spoken to each other much except during designated class time began to sit together, share a laugh before and after class, and reach out to one another during the discussions. Body language grew more relaxed. There was more good-natured joking and helping each other out intellectually during class time. We began to feel more like a team.

I'll address the benefits related to empathy and ethical behavior more in Chapter 7, but I want to highlight one last point about Jack here, and that is this: not only can it be difficult for students to feel empathy for one another when they are frustrated by each other's behavior, but it can be difficult for teachers to feel empathy, too.

Jack pushed every button I had. He regularly spouted off ideas that I objected to politically and morally. He liked to provoke, so he was an expert at figuring out what teachers' and peers' buttons were and how to push them. He would say things that I often found offensive and I grew frustrated that none of the young women in the class seemed to stand up for their gender in discussions when he said things like, "feminists are just angry, unattractive women." Because he was loud and adamant, nobody really countered anything he had to say, though I was aware that there were students in the class who disagreed with him. To put it bluntly, I wanted him out of my class because he ran counter to my beliefs on most issues and he really got under my skin. The only way forward was to push through the pain. Going back to the drawing board several times for a student who really irked me wasn't necessarily pleasant in the moment, but it taught me an important lesson about patience. Early in my career, Jack would have derailed the whole class. Or worse, perhaps I would have condescended to him, schooling him publicly in feminist philosophy or engaging in an intellectual *tête-à-tête,* winning the battle but ultimately losing the war. Instead, Spider Web Discussion became a tool for me to draw upon my patience, creativity, and empathy to turn a volatile situation into a calmer, more productive one.

What the Research Says

I have noticed a pattern in student behavior: bad, defiant, emotional, difficult, or hostile student behavior is always a symptom of a serious problem in the home. Perhaps it's because I'm married to a clinical psychologist who has worked as a school counselor for many years, but I am very aware of the connection between students' behavior and problems in their personal lives. I experienced this in my first teaching job at a rural boarding school in New England. One of my 10th grade students, a girl I'll call Meredith, typified entitled, privileged, behavior. She was smart-alecky, a little sneaky, and complained about anything that required her effort if she didn't want to give it. Most teachers would have labeled her a spoiled brat.

Halfway through the year, she experienced a family crisis. I recall her sitting on the sofa in the dorm, sobbing uncontrollably. Gone was the attitude and the bluster; instead, she bared herself as authentic and vulnerable, recounting how guilty she felt about the family crisis, describing how bitter her parents' divorce had become, and confessing her fear about her father's addiction to drugs. That's a lot of weight for a 15-year-old girl to carry around. Suddenly, I understood where her bratty behavior arose from—it was her attempt to control the chaos in her life.

Since that moment, I have seen a 100 percent correlation between bad student behavior and serious personal problems. Time and time again, I'd hear about a dreaded student coming my way from someone else's class (usually a high school boy), a student who is notorious for aggressive, lazy, or defiant behavior. As I got to know the student, I'd learn there were alarming red flags in the student's life: divorces and custody battles, parental drug or alcohol abuse, child abuse, the death of a parent or sibling. In the midst of these kinds of crises, students may not want or be able to sit down and pay attention to a lecture on macroeconomics or study for a test on the preterite versus the imperfect in Spanish. And a repeated pattern of those responses raises academic red flags that we should always be attentive to, causing us to ask: what else might be going on here?

Two of my own stories elucidate this notion. When I was a sophomore in high school, my mother became ill and my family situation began to deteriorate rapidly; it was not a happy home. My *A-* average in Spanish dropped to a *C+* in one quarter. I began failing several assignments in a subject I had traditionally loved and given a lot of time and attention to. I vividly remember that no one ever asked me why, or if anything was going on at home. Rather, I got a stern lecture from my Spanish teacher and a warning from my advisor that I'd better get my grades up if I wanted to get into a good college. I never had a chance to speak to anyone about the anguish I was experiencing in my personal life because no one asked.

The second story highlights how we often apply a double standard to students that we don't hold ourselves (emotionally mature adults) to. I was devastated by the unexpected death of my father in May 2015. When I went back to work for the final three weeks of the school year, I could barely function. I couldn't stop crying in my office during the school day and sometimes had to go to the restroom to wash my face before meetings so colleagues and students wouldn't know the state I was in. I thought back to the many students over the years who had returned after bereavement leave for the death of a parent or sibling. I realized how hard it must have been for them to go about their day, doing homework and socializing as if nothing had happened. I myself failed to do that at the age of 37, and I was suddenly flooded with empathy for all the students— no matter how bratty or difficult—that had gone through it before me, students I probably hadn't supported nearly enough in the ways they had needed.

I share these personal anecdotes to highlight how we need to be very aware of our students' emotional lives, especially when challenges arise in the classroom. Young children and adolescents act out their behavior in more mysterious ways than most adults. In most cases, they have not learned the emotional vocabulary or maturity to describe their pain, frustration, or anger, and so instead might behave in ways that bewilder or infuriate us.

The problem is particularly pronounced for boys. Think of the "Jacks" in your life, the students who most aggravated you or disrupted your classroom. I bet most of them have been boys. Psychologist and school speaker Michael Thompson (2004) specializes in the behavior of boys and what makes them so challenging to teach. He often refers to the unique challenges of education today, where a young boy can go through elementary school and never have a male teacher or adult role model in his world at school. The environment is decidedly "feminized," offering many more women teachers and rule-setters than men, and valuing students who sit still, remain quiet, and focus on the task at hand, which is often easier for girls than for boys. Thompson discusses this challenge:

> By school age, three-quarters of the boys in a class are more physically active, more impulsive and developmentally immature in comparison to girls the same age. Our average boy is also one to two years behind the average girl in his language development and reading. (p. 28)

When I introduce Spider Web Discussion, there is always a core group of boys whose faces light up, who seem switched on and engaged for the first time in my class. Many of them love having a voice, especially in the typical high school where, unfortunately, it's possible to go through a whole day and not speak once during a class. Many love that they can debate ideas and be an active participant instead of a passive listener.

Thompson further highlights thoughts on the nature of boys and why they tend to clash with teachers or peers in traditional school settings. He maintains that boys challenge us because they often are interested in things that to us seem rude or crude—they want to read *Captain Underpants*, and we want them to read something more literary.

Thompson's assessment may have seemed extreme to me as an educator until I had my own two boisterous boys and realized the influence of the school system on them. I understood viscerally that many boys (and some girls) are born with a need to move and make noise. They cannot help it. They do not feel that they are being rude. They are not trying to annoy you. They are just being themselves. Once I saw these traits so clearly in my own sons from the time they were very young, I began to adapt my own classroom to make it more boy friendly. I installed a Nerf basketball hoop on my classroom door and allowed any student to shoot hoops or challenge others to free-throw contests to pass time between classes. In my 90-minute blocks, I allow a five-minute break and stretch during which students could move, shoot hoops, or chat with a class-mate. The goal of these brain-breaks wasn't to make the classroom more fun or inviting, though I think that was one result, but to improve focus and morale in those classes. I had more patience and room for "boy" behavior, and in turn they had more patience for me when I wanted them to engage in a long activity.

Thompson raises a critical issue, not only for ELA teachers but for all teachers who assign reading: many school-sanctioned texts are boring. If we want students, particularly reluctant readers, to engage, we need to assign engaging texts. Yet, I think we educators, particularly in upper grades, have too rigid an idea of what constitutes worthy reading in our classrooms. If the goal is good critical thinking and communication, we can reach that goal whether we assign Chaucer's *Canterbury Tales* or the graphic novel *Persepolis*. I can tell you with certainty that my students' critical thinking and discussion skills are far enhanced by a text they consider engaging. I've had riveting, high-level dis-cussions on articles like the two I cited in Chapter 3, on Gareth Hinds's graphic novel version of Homer's *The Odyssey*, on films like *Princess Mononoke* or *The Truman Show* that detail Joseph Campbell's "hero's journey," and even on an analysis of the evolution of diction and tone in Jay-Z's rap lyrics. One of the best, simplest ways to reach out to a defiant or challenging student is to offer a text he really connects to and wants to say something about. I have found that to be half the battle.

The choice of text isn't only about boredom with teacher-centric literature; it can also be an issue of equity. According to the National Center for Education Statistics, the majority of U.S. teachers are white: for the 2011–2012 school year, 82 percent of public school teachers and 88 percent of private school teachers were non-Hispanic white (Goldring, Gray, & Bitterman, 2013). Yet, as the center notes in their May 2017 report: "The number of White students enrolled in public schools is projected to continue decreasing between fall 2014 and fall 2026 (from 24.9 million to 23.4 million). In 2026, White students are expected to account for 45 percent of total enrollment" (NCES, 2017).

Research shows that student engagement increases when culturally relevant texts are assigned, but many white educators may not have as much experience or knowledge of texts that aren't from the more traditional canon or weren't books we read or studied ourselves. In one small study of African American males at private school, the findings showed an increase in student engagement when culturally relevant texts and dialectical journals (referred to here as "double-entry journals") were assigned (Patterson, 2012).

Although the study was too small (only nine participants) to draw many conclusions, it makes sense and speaks to my own experience with text choice and using dialectical journals as a way to further engage students in the process of Spider Web Discussion.

In a 2006 article in the journal *Multicultural Education*, English Language Learning teacher Mary-Virginia Feger writes how important culturally relevant literature is to her predominantly Latin American students and their success in becoming readers. She determined that her students needed "access to literature that offered characters and problems similar to their own lives and identities" (Feger, 2006, p. 18).

Overall, Spider Web Discussion will offer challenges and triumphs for you as a teacher that are part of the package of learning and growth, both for you and your students. However, when you have a particularly challenging situation on your hands, the research supports creating optimal safety conditions in your classroom, which includes an environment friendly to girls and boys, and texts that speak to young people of varied interest, ability, and background.

Practical Considerations

Being a teacher means being a master of many skill sets. For example, I found that I used psychology far more in my job as a high school English teacher than I ever would have imagined. Being able to read the room and know your

students' individual personalities, as well as your own, and how they will interact is an important part of being an effective teacher or administrator. The
first and foremost priority in Spider Web Discussion is creating a safe, inclusive
learning environment for you and the students. Often, this atmosphere is easy
to achieve with a list of clear criteria and practice. But other times you will find
that just one or two personalities can shift the entire balance and upset you
or other students to such a degree that productive discussion is stymied and
you will have to work hard to strategize ways to find equilibrium. When you
encounter these challenging situations, try to ask yourself three questions that
will help you decide your next steps:

- What is the end goal? What do I want to achieve with these students and
  this discussion method?
- What kind of personalities, background experience, and life stories are in
  play here? Who is clashing or disrupting, and why do I think that might be?
- Given the answers to the above two questions, what is the best way forward? What immediate steps can I take to build bridges and keep discussion calm, productive, and focused on the goals?

Sometimes we have such a negative experience with a group of students
that we lose perspective and perhaps even control. One of my former colleagues,
a veteran teacher with a phenomenal rapport with students, had the worst
classroom experience of her career—after teaching for 15 years. Her classroom
was a toxic mix: new students who had been accepted to the school despite very
low achievement at previous schools and who weren't familiar with the high
standards for behavior and academic honesty, several students with learning
disabilities (including dyslexia) who did not receive any official support for their
learning needs because the school did not provide it, and a classroom makeup
of 80 percent boys and 20 percent girls. The result was the worst behavior she
had seen in the classroom, surely driven by students who felt overwhelmed by
the academic demands they could not keep up with and did not have support
for. These students acted out their frustrations via disrespectful, disruptive
behavior on a daily basis.

In a situation like this, there are more pressing concerns than whether
students are referencing the text regularly during a discussion. Teachers and

students alike need to feel safe and supported in their classrooms. When you have an extreme situation such as the one described here, you need help. I recommend reaching out to colleagues and administrators to help problem solve and restore calm so that all your students have a chance to learn. In this colleague's case, she invited the dean of students to observe her class every day for several weeks, which helped set a tone for the behavior and offered clear consequences for those who were distracting from the learning time.

Less extreme cases of bad behavior or personality clashes in your class can also be alleviated by getting an outside perspective. If you are struggling beyond what you feel is normal during collaborative time, invite outside observers, critical friends, or students from other classes to observe and give you (and perhaps the whole class) feedback. Just having someone new in the room sends a signal to students to "up their game." If the undesirable behavior continues when the observer is no longer in the room, invite the observer (or a series of observers) to come regularly to watch discussion and provide open feedback after each visit. Sometimes an outside voice can alleviate some of the bad chemistry in a given group, and often provides you, the teacher, with some fresh perspective as well.

Advanced Applications

Once you have a level of comfort and familiarity with the process of Spider Web Discussion, you might want to introduce roles from time to time. I don't use them every day because I think they can feel a little prescribed. With Jack's class, it became necessary to have roles during every discussion, especially when we needed to create greater balance. As we started to achieve that balance, I eased off the roles, using one or two or occasionally using them all.

Spider Web Discussion Roles

I'll explain some of the roles that I have come up with over the years. This is not a definitive or extensive list; feel free to adapt or add to it as you see fit. One teacher in a workshop I gave described how he had adapted roles to fit some of the most prominent philosophies in his actual philosophy course. For example, if the class plan was to debate a particular ethical or world issue, he assigned students roles like Karl Marx, Socrates, and Elizabeth Cady Stanton in order to have them prepare and discuss the issues and texts from those figures' philosophical lenses. The most important point about using roles is that they should be paths that help the students reach the rubric goals.

Web Grapher: Graphs the conversation web. Circles the name of the student who starts, then draws a line from the first student who talks to the next. Continues doing this to graph the "web."

3-Question Asker: Asks three, and only three, questions during the entire discussion. They must be very thoughtful questions that aim to spark new or better discussion. Cannot speak aside from asking the three questions.

Key Passage Leader: Identifies the 2–4 key parts of the text that need to be discussed and analyzed. They may be chosen for their key plot points or their analytical merit. These are the passages that are key to the plot and understanding of the text—the big moments. (Can be helpful to assign this role in advance.)

Textual Evidence Leader: Keeps the discussion firmly rooted in the text. As people discuss, the Textual Evidence Leader tries to find the quote to support the point being discussed, or prompts the speaker to do so. If the class does this well on their own, the TEL may not need to prompt much, but the person filling the role is there to remind the class that they need to refer to the text to support their comments.

Rubric Leader: In charge of the rubric and the big picture of what's happening in the discussion. Helps people accomplish their given roles by prompting them if need be, reminding them that they haven't done x, y, or z as a group yet. May only speak once or twice near the middle or end of discussion to get the class focused on the goals.

Host: Invites students to the discussion who are silent and have not yet participated much or at all. Hosts should aim to be a "good host" and offer less intimidating, easier questions to their "guests," as being put on the spot is stressful. A question like, "What did you think, Jamie?" might seem easy but is often too vague for a shy student to tackle well. Worse, the student may not have been attentive and has been caught not knowing what is currently being discussed. So the Host is encouraged to learn to ask questions like, "Do you think he's trustworthy as a character? Why not?" or "Why do you think she lies to her mother?" or "What do you like the most about this book? The least? Why?"

Vocabulary/Literary Terms Leader: Charged with having a hard copy of the current vocabulary and literary terms we're working on as a class and making sure that at least one new one is used at least once during the discussion, either by him or someone else in the class.

Feedback Giver: The only student who is silent the whole class and is not expected to talk (i.e., cannot talk). The job of this student is to have a copy of the discussion rubric and to take notes throughout the whole discussion on what worked well and what didn't. The Feedback Giver speaks only when the discussion has ended and the debriefing begins. The Web Grapher shows the graph of the discussion and the Feedback Giver then proceeds to share her observations.

If you teach younger students, consider using roles the way Shannon uses them in her 2nd grade classroom—students are tasked with using little cards with words or symbols on them that they hold up to alert each other when the discussion is going off topic, when students aren't listening, or when interruptions happen.

Voices from the Field

—BETH DAGITSES, ENGLISH TEACHER, INTERNATIONAL SCHOOL OF ESTONIA, TALLINN, ESTONIA—Introducing Spider Web Discussion to my 9th grade class was a piece of cake. The older class, on the other hand, was a bit more skeptical about this method of discussion for textual analysis. I was new to the school, and this class in particular was made up of a quirky bunch I'd inherited in the second year of a two-year program. They ranged from 16 to 19 years old, weren't exactly a united class, and were used to a traditional teaching style. They were quite far behind in the curriculum, and knew this, so the prospect of learning how to do a Spider Web Discussion seemed irrelevant and worthless to them. From their perspective, they just needed me to tell them what devices the author used to deliver her message.

Having tried Spider Web Discussion once or twice with disastrous results, I decided to find out what the problem was via a set of reflective questions focused on metacognition, as this would give me an idea of what they understood about the process and what needed further practice or explanation. To say their responses were overwhelmingly negative would be an understatement. Not only did they see it as a complete waste of time, it was clear they'd put up a block on giving it a fair try. In fact, they were angry about having to do Spider Web Discussion in general.

I wanted to give up. I also felt the time crunch kicking in, and I started to second-guess myself and my ability to help them succeed. Yes, I could simply lecture during every class, but I knew in my heart this wasn't what was best for them. The skills they would develop as a result of Spider Web Discussion—critical thinking, communication, collaboration, and self-management—were in fact the very skills they needed to succeed in their upcoming oral assessment and beyond their last year of high school.

During our next class, I reiterated these truths to them. I detailed explicitly how these skills would benefit them in the future and insisted I wasn't giving up on them and the Spider Web Discussion. I asked them to forget the idea of grades, exams, anything negative that had happened in the past, and just go with the flow; to use one another and this discussion as a means for finding out more about the text; to see it as a risk-free zone, one of safety, where they could feel free to ask their burning questions, and be willing and eager to help their peers understand the nuances of the writer's craft.

We tried our next discussion with assigned roles for certain students. Some of the more vocal students were given roles that limited their participation to only asking three questions. Another role was to provide feedback about how the discussion was going so the students could alter its direction if needed. One student was given the role of host and was tasked with ensuring a balance of responses and keeping the discussion moving.

To their credit, the students gave this format a chance. But again, their feedback told me they were still worried. What if they missed some vital piece of information? What if someone said something wrong? What if the most important aspect of the text wasn't covered and then they never even knew about it? This is when I realized that these students didn't feel confident as inquirers. It was clear they didn't believe in themselves and felt they wouldn't succeed if left to their own devices. The next class started with me explaining to them that their take on a given text was as important as those of scholars. And more often than not, someone in the class would bring up more scholarly observations.

Still, they were skeptical. So I made a deal with them. Just like in the game show, "Who Wants to Be a Millionaire," I agreed to let them phone a friend—the friend being me. If at any point during the discussion they weren't sure about something, they were allowed to ask me for clarification—up to three times in a single Spider Web Discussion. This option allayed their fears and they were ready to take on the next text.

We engaged in several more Spider Web Discussions, each subsequent attempt better than the last. A few weeks later, it was time to officially assess the class on their Spider Web Discussion. Though there was still room for improvement, this class was finally seeing the benefits. It was a struggle but the students started to demonstrate the skills of critical thinkers, communicators, and collaborators, and their first-ever graded Spider Web Discussion was a success.

For the record, they never actually "phoned" me. Somehow just knowing they could was enough.

Big Takeaway

The majority of the time, students take to Spider Web Discussion quickly and enthusiastically, despite the typical growing pains of learning a new method and assessment system. From time to time, however, you may have a group or an individual who stumps or frustrates you, making you feel like the method may not work for that particular class.

Again, I'll bring you back to my favorite phrase when I present on Spider Web Discussion: *like writing, it's a process*. We expect all students to learn to write and improve upon their writing skills over the course of their K–12 education.

We don't allow students to opt out of learning how to write due to personalities, interest level, or even disabilities like dyslexia. Instead, we challenge ourselves to innovate new and better ways to engage students in the skill and help them hone it. When I adopted this approach with Spider Web Discussion, it became much easier to accept my role in helping students like Jack and his peers figure out how to address challenges with the method to a more positive, productive end point. It's about adaptability.

The opening vignette, Rob's story, is based on a real situation that happened to a colleague of mine. He was very frustrated by "Adam's" behavior and did not want to abandon a method that clearly produced results for the class as a whole despite the one individual student's performance. After Rob spoke with Adam one on one and got nowhere, he turned to me for advice. He was worried about the dynamic of the group grade when one student was refusing to participate. And if the rest of the class was penalized in the group grade by his malicious behavior, then it also didn't seem fair. Together, we decided that the goal was to continue to have strong, productive discussions that, eventually, Adam might join. Given that, we decided it was fair to exclude him from the assessment process entirely until he wanted to participate. He would get an "I" in the grade book, a no-count grade that signaled his lack of participation, and the rest of the class received the no-count grade for that day's discussion. Adam was told that when he was ready to participate in the discussions, he could participate in the grade, and in the meantime, he would have to explain to his parents what the "I" meant in the grade book and why it was there if they asked. This would likely prompt him to reconsider his opt-out stance. Rob was pleased when we came up with this strategy, as he really hadn't wanted to abandon a method that seemed to be working despite this one recalcitrant student. Eventually, Adam came around and did participate from time to time. The power of positive peer pressure and the desire to belong can work greatly in your favor when using a team-building method like Spider Web Discussion. Don't be afraid to innovate, adapt, and keep seeking the results you are looking for. Where there is a will, there is a way, even with your most challenging student.

6 ASSESSMENT IS A TOOL, NOT A WEAPON

Marisol had heard about Spider Web Discussion from Ahmed and was intrigued by his enthusiasm for the method. She met with Ahmed to go over the basics of Spider Web Discussion and to learn how to introduce it to her class. She was especially struck by the group grade, which was something counter to the grading philosophies that she learned through her master's program studies and her own classroom experience. In her experience, group grades nearly always resulted in one student doing the work while others dragged down the grade or piggy-backed on it, and this didn't seem fair to Marisol. Ahmed insisted, though, that the group grade didn't "count" and that the method was working wonders for his class. She wondered how seriously the students would take an activity with a formative, no-count grade. She had had trouble with that kind of thing in the past, but Ahmed was excited about how well it was working in his class and she decided to give it a try.

When she introduced the method to the class, she did it as Ahmed advised: she showed her students video footage of an actual Spider Web Discussion from another school, handed out the rubric, and discussed it with the students. "Please note the group grade," she announced as they were looking over the rubric's criteria. "This means you all sink, or you all swim. So be careful, one of you can really bring down the grade for the rest of the class, even if it doesn't 'count.'" Marisol was thinking of one student in particular. Evan had behavior problems and didn't do much of the reading for the class; he seemed happy to fail the reading quizzes and take the low grades, despite her best efforts. She was pretty sure he wouldn't help at all with the group grade, especially since it was a no-count grade. Where was his incentive?

Then, as Ahmed had encouraged her to, she sat in the back on an extra desk in the corner so she could see everyone clearly from a slight height. She diagrammed the web and took notes while the students discussed the homework reading—a section from *Jane Eyre*—for 40 minutes.

It didn't go well.

Only a few students spoke most of the time, and some of the students, the shyer ones, didn't get into the discussion at all. It wound up being a discussion among her smartest, most diligent students while the others listened or daydreamed. Evan was off task for much of the discussion; it was clear he hadn't done the reading and didn't have much to say. He kept flicking his pencil and sighing with boredom.

During the debrief Marisol showed students the graph of the discussion, which the students observed with interest. She stood at the front of the classroom and asked them to assess each criteria on the rubric one by one. "Go through each one and simply answer the question of whether we did this, yes or no." When the students assessed themselves according to the rubric, Marisol was a little surprised that they agreed with her—it had been a *D* or *D+* discussion when they took into account all the criteria. She addressed the class in a disappointed voice: "Some of you did all the talking, and many others didn't get in there at all today, but equal talk time is the very first thing on the rubric. You need to do better if you want a better grade. As I said, it's a team effort to discuss this way." She paced back and forth a little. "And it's clear that some of you aren't even up to date with the reading." She eyed Evan, and most of the class noticed. "C'mon, guys. You're letting your team down."

Marisol felt discouraged; she had worried about this from the beginning. Maybe Ahmed had a great group of students who were just naturally inclined to this kind of method, but it didn't seem like this was going to work for her class.

The question I get asked the most is about that elephant in the room: the group grade.

When I first began using Spider Web Discussion, I simply followed the unofficial school protocol: a certain percentage of students' grades was based on participation, and participation grades were mostly derived from our discussions because the school was a Harkness school. Neither parents nor students complained about it because everyone understood that this was the school's philosophy. The grading "fairness" issue never came up. We counted group grades in this way, and no one at that school seemed to have a problem with that structure.

After that school, I went to work at an international school with incredibly strict curriculum and assessment policies. I was to teach the same material and carry out the same lesson on the same day as my colleagues who taught the same courses that I did. All assessments had to be common across the course and given on the same day, where possible. For every major assessment, the teachers graded (or "moderated" in IB parlance) a sample together to make sure we were grading the same way. For every course we taught, we had a weekly team meeting in which we planned the upcoming week and aligned our assessments. This meant, of course, that I could definitely not count the Spider Web grades I had come to see as the backbone of the method. I worried that without a group grade that counted and factored into students' GPAs, there was little chance of producing the authentic collaboration and civility I had seen blossom in my classroom in the years prior. When I voiced my concern to a colleague in a meeting early in the year, she quipped, "Well, you can still use that method. Just don't count the grade."

This was a new concept. I had my doubts. *After all,* I thought, *if students weren't rewarded with the carrots of grades, why would they even bother to make the effort or do the work?* But I didn't really have a choice. My options at that school were to use Spider Web Discussion with a formative, no-count grade or not at all, because no one else was going to use the method in their courses that year. So no-count grade it was.

I discovered quickly that whether the grade counted or not didn't make a difference. I didn't notice a change in participation, homework completion, or quality of discussion in these students. They treated the rubric, the symbolic grade, and the collaborative process as seriously as my previous students had.

Now, I'll be completely honest: that first year with a no-count grade, I didn't advertise that it was symbolic up front. I simply gave the same pitch I always gave at the beginning of the year when I introduced Spider Web Discussion, explaining the rubric and mentioning that there would be a group grade. The grade never showed up in their grade books or transcripts that year, and none of the students ever questioned it. Many of them probably assumed it was being factored into their total average, although the breakdown on the syllabus showed all the percentages and Spider Web Discussion was not one of them.

But the experience taught me something very important, which was that I could tweak the assessment model without adversely affecting the outcome. So in subsequent years, I tweaked further. When I wound up at a different international school in Malaysia, I found myself bound to a policy that prohibited group grades. I petitioned to be able to use the group grade for Spider Web Discussion as a small percentage of students' participation grade based on the specific aims of the method, which focuses on improving group work and collaboration, and was granted that permission as long as I clearly advised parents and students in my course syllabus. I made it clear there would be no group grades for projects or presentations, which is what most students and parents object to. Instead, the group grade was an assessment and feedback mechanism on the skill of collaboration itself, something we were aiming to improve in the course. There were zero complaints that year or the following year about the group grade from my more than 80 students or their parents.

A few years later, when I found myself at a school that highly valued non-weighted formative assessment (that is to say: the grade goes in the electronic grade book for parents and students to see, but it is not factored into the overall average at all—it has a weight of 0 percent), I saw new possibilities for Spider Web Discussion. In this new system, most of the discussion we had was for formative grades, accumulating over time in the grade book as a clear pattern for all to see but not "counting" toward the students' overall averages.

Having experimented with a variety of assessment formats for Spider Web Discussion, I now believe that the most powerful, pedagogically sound use of it is through formative, no-count group grades. There are two reasons for my belief. First, I think the group grade is crucial because it's an issue of backward design: what outcomes are we seeking with this kind of discussion method and classroom philosophy? Ethical, balanced, high-level, shared inquiry. If those are the outcomes, then an assessment structure that asks students to participate in, get feedback on, and self-assess those outcomes makes sense. Therefore, the group grade makes sense as the mechanism for feedback on the quality of the group collaboration. Spider Web Discussion is nothing like the group project where one person does all the work and the other student gets the grade. That is really a misuse of an individual grade, because students are pooling their time and resources to produce a single project that is assessed individually. In those cases, it is often difficult or impossible to assess students accurately as individuals. Spider Web Discussion is different in aim and purpose. It is a collective activity and is assessed in order to give feedback on the quality of the collective work. The method allows for feedback on individuals' contributions through coding, but the grading and feedback overall are meant to be tailored to the specific desired outcome of *effective collaborative inquiry*. If the method is paired with individual Dialectical Journal or other individual assessments that evince clear patterns of individual skills and knowledge, the group discussion grade in no way clouds the teacher's, students', or parents' understanding of individual students' achievement. Instead, it provides valuable feedback on how well the group is working together *as a group* at any one point in time.

The second reason I believe the no-count group grade is the most sound and powerful approach to assessing Spider Web Discussion is because we need to move away from the notion that students will only perform effectively when there are carrots and sticks. Many arts, P.E., technical, and vocational teachers know this to be true already. In subject areas that are product-based, culminating in a piece of art, a performance, a game situation, or a project, students often have an intrinsic motivation that they don't have in more academic subjects that focus on skills and assessments without a clear or finished goal from the student's perspective. An example of this in action: I was part of an instructional round a few years ago in which an IB higher-level math teacher and an IB physics teacher visited the IB visual arts teacher's room to see what might be learned from her classroom. Both the math and physics teacher were amazed by the level of autonomy they witnessed. Students were working entirely on their own on separate projects without chaos or inappropriate behavior. Both teachers expressed envy that the subject of art seemed to intrinsically motivate the students in a way that the straight content of their courses did not. An interesting follow-up, though: the physics teacher was determined to experiment with the visual arts approach in his classroom after seeing it in action and designed physics experiments in "centers" around his room, much like he had seen in the art class. He reported satisfaction with the result and a desire to continue experimenting more with this type of product-based learning.

The teacher can also enhance motivation by holding students to high collaboration standards via the rubric, treating the group grade as vital feedback to be taken seriously. We do this not by treating the grade as a weapon with which to discourage or punish students, as the fictional Marisol does in the opening vignette. We use it as an indicator of how well students collaborate. They want to be prepared for their future academic challenges and careers, and if you sell them on the positive benefits of collaboration and group assessment through warm but firm feedback, you will find them motivated during Spider Web Discussions despite grades that don't count.

Ultimately, if we want students to collaborate authentically, why don't we design work that really assesses that skill? Assigning a group project does not achieve that aim. Holding a Socratic seminar in which the teacher directs the conversation does not achieve that aim. But Spider Web Discussion with a rubric that demands ethical behavior, autonomy, and a team mentality does. A discussion with an individual grade just doesn't achieve the same thing because by nature students are competing against each other for air time and to see who can say the brightest, most insightful thing. When there are individual grades, they do not listen to each other as well, they do not build on each other's arguments, as they are too focused on what they need to get out in order to get the grade.

I also don't allow students to get away with saying to each other, "oh, don't worry. It doesn't even count." The few times I hear comments like this, I respond by saying kindly, "just because you aren't rewarded for something with an external prize doesn't mean it doesn't count. We are building something here and we are working hard together to find meaning and grow as thinkers and team players. Just like your soccer or basketball practice, every minute counts because we have a chance to be better and learn from our mistakes or let that opportunity slip away. Let's not let it slip away. We are all counting on you."

And that is one of the keys to Spider Web Discussion: it's treating kids as vital, equal partners in this process. It's showing them that their voice, behavior, and questions matter. If you can show each of them you believe in them and hold them to high standards in this regard, you can get buy-in from even the most cynical or unmotivated students. To do this effectively, you must be very aware of two things: your power and your approach.

First let's talk about power, an even bigger elephant in the room than group grades. At the root of the anxiety students and their parents feel about grades is the power dynamic. Rightly or not, most students view the teacher as having the power to help or hurt them on their path to success through the grades the teacher "gives" them. Although most teachers view grading as something students earn fair and square, many students do not feel this way, particularly in classes like English or history, where there seem to be fewer right or wrong answers as there are in math. This can lead to students who feel that the teacher "just doesn't like her" or will give her writing a C every time "just because it's her." I used to be very unsympathetic to this line of thinking when I was in my first 10 years of teaching, but one experience in particular changed this for me.

That event was a series of days I spent shadowing students based on the recommendation of my principal. At my father's urging, I blogged about the experience for his education blog. The post hit a nerve and went viral and wound up being reprinted around the world in various newspapers and magazines. You can see a clear summary and the original copy in the *Washington Post*, cited in the bibliography (Strauss, 2014). One of the big takeaways I had from that eye-opening experience was how much students feel like cattle. It probably isn't intentional from the adults or the institution, but over four days of shadowing, I felt as if the adults in the community were rushing us around, annoyed by our questions, and constantly asking us to sit down and be quiet. Let me be clear—the teachers were doing their jobs as they were expected to and as I had done up to that point: get the students into class, get them settled, get them to work, keep them on task, get them out the door to their next engagement when the bell rings. But when you are actually one of those students, the feeling is totally different. You feel the power dynamic much more clearly. The teacher stands, you sit. The teacher talks, you listen. The teacher instructs or hands out an assessment, you take notes or take the test. If we needed to go to the bathroom, we asked for permission. If we needed another pencil during a test, we asked for permission. If we had a question when the teacher had already moved on from the point, we asked our tablemate at the risk of seeming off task and getting called out for it. I was very conscious that I was on the other side of the power dynamic.

That first day shadowing a student, I understood that I needed to change the way I related to students to reach them more effectively. For example, I would make an effort to treat them with greater kindness and with more respect, and to act as less of an authority figure. As a parent, I'm constantly telling my own children yes or no all day long, guiding them toward what they can and can't do based on my husband's and my long-term goals for their safety and learning. Most parents do the same, which means that most of our students are spending nearly all their waking hours being told what to do and when and how to do it by the adults in their life. This is just a reality of life as a young person, but I realized through my experience that if my goal was to create engaged, autonomous learners, then I would immediately need to shift the power dynamic so it felt much more balanced to the students. If they feel bossed around at home and school all day, they lose intrinsic motivation and engagement. They tune out. They feel left out of the system in which they spend most of their waking hours.

One thing I changed to consciously shift the power dynamic was through sitting and standing time. When I am sitting with the students, at the oval table, and we can all see each other's faces, I am equal with them. I'm communicating to them that we are all on the same level intellectually. It's OK that it might not be entirely true (I almost certainly know more about the subject I teach than they do), but I am giving them the impression that I think of them as intellectual equals, thereby earning their trust. I'm showing them through my body language that I don't think myself above them, that I am part of the team effort. I never debrief a Spider Web Discussion when standing up and I never stand over them or sit above them on a desk during the discussion itself, even if I want to see better. For the discussion itself, I sit at the same style desk or table they do, in the back, away from them so I am not their focus. During the debrief, I pull up a chair in between two students at their circle and I make myself just one of many at the table. It is during the debrief that the grade is determined (first by the students, then with my feedback and input) and it's very important that the teacher be seated as a team member during this moment to even out the power dynamic of the grading process.

You may have noticed Marisol in the opening vignette did neither of these things, and I wouldn't have expected her to without training or a shadowing experience like I had, but I share her fictional story as a cautionary tale to teachers: you may need to confront some uncomfortable truths about power, authority, and autonomy in your classroom in order to see Spider Web Discussion be as successful as it can be.

A second change I made as a result of shadowing is that I go out of my way to be as kind, warm, and friendly as I can during class time. Sometimes I lose my patience. Sometimes stern talk is called for. But on most days, I try to make every single student who walks through my door feel that they are welcome and wanted there in our classroom. You may have noted that Marisol wasn't particularly kind during her debrief, probably due to her frustration; she singled out Evan publicly, embarrassing him in front of his peers and further isolating a student who she was already having difficulty reaching. When you introduce Spider Web Discussion, imagine you are introducing it to a group of very young students—such as kindergarteners—and apply the same approach you would with them: be a smiling, kind friend and ally, not a wielder of power. Many middle school and high school teachers (including me) grow frustrated with the apathy, the grade-grubbing, the cheating, and the classroom behavior we experience. But I have seen some of the worst students in schools transform into engaged, respectful peers during discussions or other classroom activities when teachers approach them with genuine kindness. My philosophy: *when in doubt, be kind*. We all have students (like Jack in Chapter 5) who annoy us and get under our skin. Quite often it can be because they remind us of ourselves when we were students and we are impatient for them to learn the lessons that we learned the hard way. Sometimes it's a student who is out of control and cannot see how her own impulses are affecting the rest of the class, or she does see it and enjoys the power. This student may have a history and needs we are unaware of, and we can never reach her or help her reach her potential if we shut her out. We all have those students we can't stand; the trick is that we need to be so good at our job that not only do these difficult students not know that we find them difficult, but in fact, they actually feel cared for and respected by us. Kindness goes a long way, so I urge you to smile and exude warmth, to sit and stand mindfully, and to err on the side of empathy, especially when it comes to debriefing and assessing Spider Web Discussion. It is, after all, the very behavior we are looking to produce and assess through the discussions and we must consistently model it for our students or they will see right through the game.

Finally, please remember that the grade itself should always be thought of as a tool for achieving your goals, not a weapon for wielding when the goals haven't yet been achieved. A group grade is a delicate thing and it requires a lot of trust, both from teacher to student and among the students themselves. Explain kindly that its use is to achieve some specific aims for group work and intellectual thinking. It's meant to push us all to higher levels of behavior and thought.

If there is already a lack of trust between teacher and students or among students themselves, you will need to address it. The group grade will not address it for you, and it will likely make it worse. You are the coach helping the students work toward winning the race. You are not the judge, nor the star player. You are a mentor and a guide. You are on their side. You want to trust them and help them lead in-depth discussions on their own, and they want to trust that you are there to help them see success. Treat the assessment as a tool toward that end and you will all reap the benefits.

And remember that the assessment process is not about assigning a grade or asking students to self-assess the grade; it's really about the feedback during the debrief. The grade is just a (no-count) value for that feedback, but the feedback itself is what indicates to students what they achieved and what still needs to be worked on. You should put more time, emphasis, and value on the feedback portion than the grade itself. I reserve about 15 minutes at the end of every discussion for high school classes in the first weeks we try the method. This time allows me to follow up on key points, debrief, ask questions, and to further probe their thinking about the text or topic. It also allows plenty of time to debrief the day's process beyond the actual grade and highlight what can be done better in the next discussion.

Marisol had her own concerns and challenges going into the introduction of Spider Web Discussion and they were amplified by her approach. Before you plan your first discussion, take a moment to reflect on the concerns or questions you have about a group grade. Perhaps you can write them down and talk them through with a trusted colleague or administrator, or maybe even the students themselves if there is a high degree of trust already. When done right, it won't feel awkward or uncomfortable for you or the students, and what's "right" for you and your class may be different than at the school down the street or on the other side of the world. Spider Web Discussion is really, at heart, a classroom ethos to which we can *all* offer something and *all* learn something from, even us teachers.

What the Research Says

Daniel Pink's 2009 book *Drive* proposes that what truly motivates humans to do their best work are autonomy, mastery, and purpose—not external carrots and sticks. "In environments where extrinsic rewards are most salient, many people work only to the point that triggers the reward—and no further. So if students get a prize for reading three books, many won't pick up a fourth, let alone embark on a lifetime of reading" (Pink, 2009, pp. 56–57).

When we apply these kind of findings to a classroom setting, we see the potential pitfalls clearly—students focused on a reward or even a grade they want to achieve may never push themselves to deeper thinking, greater challenge, or more creativity because the external motivator—the carrot—has been obtained. No teacher or school wants to see students focused only on short-term goals or only on GPA, as evinced by the mission statements of so many education institutions that profess wanting to produce "lifelong learners." What if the way we often motivate students through grades is short-sighted, producing students that stop themselves from achieving more due to already obtained carrots?

Or what if those carrots are actually producing work of limited quality? Based on another study Pink cites in his book, there may be implications for the carrot and stick approach with regard to the efficiency and quality of problem solving. Pink cites research showing that for cognitive tasks, the participants actually performed *worse* with an incentive than without one at all. What if the stress and pressure of the carrot and stick approach to grades for our students is producing opposite outcomes than the ones we desire? Might our students be limited by the way we often grade their work, particularly in the high school years? Pink offers some advice for those of us looking to inspire better, deeper work from those we work with. He suggests we consider nontangible rewards like loaded, positive feedback. The feedback should be informative and specific ("great use of color" rather than simply "great job").

Spider Web Discussion avoids the carrot and stick approach by giving a grade only as a feedback mechanism, never as a reward or a punishment. And Pink's notion that people need meaningful, specific feedback on their work makes sense to us educators who work continuously to help our students improve and know that this rarely happens without challenge and specific, targeted feedback. Spider Web Discussion offers students the chance to get that kind of feedback and act on it regularly, and it also gives them the chance to be an active participant in the feedback process so that they, too, can hone their feedback skills. Pink suggests that autonomy, mastery, and purpose are the keys to unlocking our drive. Spider Web Discussion offers students the chance to develop autonomy as they facilitate and assess their own discussions; the chance to achieve mastery as they engage in deep, critical thinking, and listening and empathy skills; and the chance to find purpose through discussing meaningful texts and finding their own voices.

Practical Considerations

The first step in assessment for Spider Web Discussion is figuring out what your specific school and district policies are with regard to assessment and designing backward from there. As I noted previously, I've adapted my assessment strategy for the method each time I've moved schools, and with each new adaptation I have learned another facet of how to assess the method. So try not to fight the system you are in. If you can report the no-count grades (which means they are seen in the grade book by students and parents but do not "count" because they are weighted 0 percent), then that is the best way to use the group grades. But if you cannot report on grades this way at all or group grades specifically, then using the grades symbolically in your own personal grade book records and your classroom alone is the next best thing.

The next step is to think through your own feelings on assessment and the needs of your class. I can't stress enough how important I believe the group grade is for the process to work effectively, so I suggest you think through your questions and concerns, write some of them down, and talk them over with colleagues and an administrator so you feel you have a sounding board and some support from your community. They might have ideas or suggestions that you hadn't thought of, such as when my principal in Malaysia agreed with using the group grade as long as it was communicated in writing to the students and parents in the syllabus.

Once you do begin the discussions and the assessment, I suggest keeping a visual record for the students to track the progress easily. For me, this means a different colored legal notepad on a clipboard for each class I teach. I keep them on a shelf where all the students can access them. They are able to flip through the pages and see the progression of the map diagrams and the grades assigned to each discussion at the end, the notes and codes I write down as they discuss. Each page is an individual discussion with a grade and brief comments, and students often like to stop and rifle through them on their way in or out of class. They sometimes like to compare their own class's work to that of another class on another clipboard. I find this demystifies the assessment process a bit for them, making it public—again, attempting to equalize that power dynamic a bit for more buy-in and student autonomy.

Lastly, just remember the phrase, *when in doubt, be kind*. The assessment process should be a tool to help you and your students reach your learning and collaboration goals. Students hear enough chiding and rules in their day-to-day lives. This is a chance to encourage and support your students. Bring them into the conversation and ask with a warm smile: "What did we do well today? What can we do better next time?"

Advanced Applications

One of the biggest benefits of graphing the discussion webs and writing down the codes next to students' names is that it gives you a wealth of feedback and data for each student that would have normally taken you many months and endless grading to accumulate. I spend about 10 minutes at the end of each day copying the codes into my grade book, so next to each name I see a pattern of codes over the weeks and months. Chandra often rambles during discussions, getting off topic. Michael regularly advances the conversation and takes it to a deeper place. Stefan is still interrupting, but much less. These data points help me have better one-to-one informal conversations with students, giving them feedback on how to improve. It also helps paint a bigger picture for me. Chandra often gets off topic in her writing as well, and so I can intervene earlier and try to make her aware of the need to follow one idea through to the end. Sometimes, the opposite is true—a student struggles mightily to communicate clear, deep ideas in his writing but comes across as perceptive, insightful, and succinct in discussions. It helps me gain a much rounder picture of each student as few students are skilled in all abilities that a subject demands. I am able to write more positive comments at the end of the term for these types of students, sharing their intellectual triumphs during discussion time and not having to focus only on the challenges of their writing. Lastly, this additional information aids in parent-teacher conferences, offering a clear pattern to discuss with parents and a path to support their child going forward.

Another advanced application that is worth considering with regard to assessment is using an iPad or tablet to graph the conversations and keep an electronic record. The app I am currently aware of that best does this is called Equity Maps, developed by an international teacher named Dave Nelson. It allows easy diagramming of the conversation map on an iPad and offers many fascinating ways to look at the data (e.g., at the push of a button, you can see how many girls spoke relative to boys and for how long). I think these kinds of applications offer advantages to teachers interested in equity in the classroom and workplace. Imagine using that tool to diagram faculty meeting talk time. The result would be illuminating.

One teacher I knew in Thailand had his STEM students design an app to track discussions. If you have the ability to teach these skills or offer an extension project to willing and curious students to create an excellent app for sale, that could be a whole additional learning experience.

Finally, many of you may be interested in Spider Web Discussion but have questions or concerns about how it fits into your school's, state's, or accrediting body's standards. Many K–12 schools have schoolwide learner profiles or principles that describe the kind of learning environment and outcomes they aim to achieve. Statements such as, "Students learn best when they are actively engaged" or "Individuals are responsible and accountable for their choices and actions" might describe the objectives of the school with regard to the kind of learning or students they hope to produce. If your school has something like this in place, it can be a useful exercise to pull out the list and do a little test against each one: Does Spider Web Discussion support this principle or aim? I find that the answer is yes for most of them. Spider Web Discussion can cover a lot of territory because it has a reach that is not merely academic. For example, it ties in with the IB Learner Profile that indicates learners are knowledgeable, caring, risk-takers, reflective, principled, communicators, inquirers, balanced, open-minded, and thinkers.

Spider Web Discussion has been referred to and promoted as one way to engage students in their IB Diploma Program's Approaches to Teaching and Learning (ATL). (Full disclosure: I worked as a consultant for the IB on their Approaches to Teaching and Learning in the DP initiative.) After my IB workshop, when participants have seen or participated in a Spider Web Discussion, I ask them to look at the learner profile and determine which of the attributes is supported by SWD. Most participants find something between 8 and 10 of them supported by Spider Web Discussion.

Many schools, both in the United States and internationally, have adopted the Common Core standards for English and Language Arts. If you teach or work in a Common Core school or state, you can rest assured that Spider Web Discussion helps achieve Common Core standards in English and even in math. Here is a list of some of the standards supported by the discussion method:

K–12 ENGLISH-LANGUAGE ART/LITERACY ANCHOR STANDARDS

Reading
Key Ideas and Details

- CCSS.ELA-Literacy.CCRA.R.1 Read closely to determine what the text says explicitly and to make logical inferences from it; cite specific textual evidence when writing or speaking to support conclusions drawn from the text.

- CCSS.ELA-Literacy.CCRA.R.2 Determine central ideas or themes of a text and analyze their development; summarize the key supporting details and ideas.

- CCSS.ELA-Literacy.CCRA.R.3 Analyze how and why individuals, events, or ideas develop and interact over the course of a text.

Craft and Structure

- <u>CCSS.ELA-Literacy.CCRA.R.4</u> Interpret words and phrases as they are used in a text, including determining technical, connotative, and figurative meanings, and analyze how specific word choices shape meaning or tone.
- <u>CCSS.ELA-Literacy.CCRA.R.5</u> Analyze the structure of texts, including how specific sentences, paragraphs, and larger portions of the text (e.g., a section, chapter, scene, or stanza) relate to each other and the whole.
- <u>CCSS.ELA-Literacy.CCRA.R.6</u> Assess how point of view or purpose shapes the content and style of a text.

Speaking and Listening Comprehension and Collaboration

- <u>CCSS.ELA-Literacy.CCRA.SL.1</u> Prepare for and participate effectively in a range of conversations and collaborations with diverse partners, building on others' ideas and expressing their own clearly and persuasively.
- <u>CCSS.ELA-Literacy.CCRA.SL.2</u> Integrate and evaluate information presented in diverse media and formats, including visually, quantitatively, and orally.
- <u>CCSS.ELA-Literacy.CCRA.SL.3</u> Evaluate a speaker's point of view, reasoning, and use of evidence and rhetoric.

K–12 STANDARDS FOR MATHEMATICAL PRACTICE

- <u>CCSS.MATH.PRACTICE.MP3</u> Construct viable arguments and critique the reasoning of others.
- Mathematically proficient students understand and use stated assumptions, definitions, and previously established results in constructing arguments. They make conjectures and build a logical progression of statements to explore the truth of their conjectures. They are able to analyze situations by breaking them into cases, and can recognize and use counterexamples. They justify their conclusions, communicate them to others, and respond to the arguments of others. They reason inductively about data, making plausible arguments that take into account the context from which the data arose. Mathematically proficient students are also able to compare the effectiveness of two plausible arguments, distinguish correct logic or reasoning from that which is flawed, and—if there

is a flaw in an argument—explain what it is. Elementary students can construct arguments using concrete referents such as objects, drawings, diagrams, and actions. Such arguments can make sense and be correct, even though they are not generalized or made formal until later grades. Later, students learn to determine domains to which an argument applies. Students at all grades can listen or read the arguments of others, decide whether they make sense, and ask useful questions to clarify or improve the arguments. (Common Core, 2010)

Voices from the Field

—KIM MCKNEE, AVONDALE HIGH SCHOOL, AUBURN HILLS, MI—

Spider Web Discussion has been a great way to present student-led peer discussion to students. The "spider" acronym clarified the goal of the web and gave them a visual for how important each student is in the process. For the first web, some students did not complete the given reading schedule and assignment so they did not get to participate in the web discussion. I gave them an alternative written assignment and no points for the group grade. By the third discussion, I had 100 percent preparedness. The first discussion was primarily text-based with few relational comments to other parts of the novel. By the fourth web discussion, most of the discussion was relational and abstract, critical thinking. The ideas and novel elements the students were able to explore without me lecturing was exciting to watch, and the classroom was more lively. Student reflections indicated they felt more inclined to complete the assignments and keep up with the reading schedule due to the expectations of their peers. I had one student track the web so I could focus on listening to the level of thinking and note things I could follow up on the next day in class.

My best advice to teachers using the SWD for the first time is to get your plan and lesson set. Watch videos to understand the process, then prepare the students with a video or diagram and the acronym. They "get it" after the first one. I had to break some of my class groups into two or three smaller webs because 30 is just too many for one discussion. One of my students requested that groups be randomly assigned so the group is more diverse and authentic.

My research partner, Jen, and I designed action research to find out the effect of Spider Web Discussion on student engagement and critical thinking. We presented together at an educational Action Research Fair for our Galileo Teacher Leader program for principals and superintendents. Our research concluded student engagement increased by 24 percent and level of critical thinking/questioning in discussion increased by 50 percent. Many people were interested in learning more about Spider Web Discussion and we have been asked to present at our high school's professional development meeting.

Big Takeaway

The key idea in this chapter is that the group grade is the backbone of the method, driving the deep, nuanced collaboration that is the goal, and that it should always be used as a tool to achieve that goal and never as a weapon. Marisol thought she was introducing Spider Web Discussion in a way that was helpful, based on a familiar power structure in the classroom—but the method requires teachers to let go of their authoritative role a bit. They can think of themselves more as coaches than judges. All teachers need to be aware of the power structures in place that may inhibit trust in the classroom between teacher and students and among students themselves, and they should actively work to equalize that power through their body language and assessment approaches so that students feel safe and secure enough to take the intellectual risks we so desire them to take. Finally, though not specifically related to assessment, one additional note on Marisol's ability to relate to students on their level: the choice of text was not exactly the most scintillating, and certainly not a recipe for success for a student like Evan. Although I love *Jane Eyre*, I always recommend a short, current, engaging film that immediately grabs the students' attention for the first discussion of the year. In this way, all students are on an equal playing field and everyone has the same chance to engage and participate, not just those who did the homework or are experienced, willing readers. When we think about getting all our students into the discussions and the best assessment strategies to do so, we also need to design backward from the best, most engaging entry points.

Finally, as we see in Kim's testimonial, even from the very first discussion and with groups as large as 30, her action-research data points to improved critical thinking, engagement, and questioning using Spider Web Discussion. It isn't a scientific study, but it echoes what I have seen in dozens of my own classes over the years and what colleagues and workshop attendees have reported to me. This type of unique assessment used thoughtfully, consistently, and kindly gets you positive results.

BENEFITS OF SPIDER WEB DISCUSSION

Liam was the odd one out in his small, close-knit class at an artsy private school. His peers were informed and cultured, versed in the language of Broadway shows and politics; Liam had a fascination with the outdoors and Greek mythology. Liam often looked grumpy, sitting with his arms crossed in front of him, eyes cast downward. He tended to be silent during discussions until some point struck him and he responded gruffly, arguing in a way that seemed a bit too intense to his slightly baffled peers. His classmates tolerated him with a benign indifference, but to adults, Liam looked socially awkward and lonely.

Kelly was a popular student and star tennis player who had gone to school with Liam since 5th grade. Academically she was good but not great. She didn't stand out in a class full of students who would wind up at Ivy League schools. She worked hard to maintain a *B* average and often felt that despite all her efforts, she would never reach the intellectual or academic heights of her peers.

Kelly had one particular skill that was brought sharply into focus during a Spider Web Discussion. Right away a clear pattern emerged: Kelly would respond to Liam's gruff outbursts with a soothing kind of summary, somehow translating his message so that the rest of the class could digest it and agree. She'd turn her whole body toward him, look directly at him with interest and enthusiasm, and say things like, "Wow, Liam, that's so true. I had never thought of it that way. You seem to be saying that Romeo is a bit of a ladies' man, a player, and that he shouldn't be trusted. I really didn't see that until you pointed it out, but it makes sense."

Kelly had a particular charm with the way she wielded her empathy, an ability to soften both Liam and the rest of the students with her genuine comments. She was the connection between Liam and the rest of the group, smoothing over awkward social encounters to create a much more unified discussion and group experience.

Kelly's teacher knew this was a particular talent that wasn't measured by traditional assessments. She had an innate knack for empathy, for sophisticated social maneuvers between groups of indifferent or even hostile peers. Kelly's teacher was glad that Spider Web Discussion had highlighted this skill for two reasons. The first was for Liam's benefit; he seemed to be able to find his place in the classroom after a couple of months of Kelly's consistent support. Second, the teacher was glad that she could give Kelly positive feedback on a high-level skill, especially when Kelly was feeling discouraged by her average reading and writing skills. The teacher began to highlight this skill for Kelly through her comments and feedback and encouraged her with comments like, "I think you'd make an incredible psychologist or social worker, Kelly. Have you ever thought about majoring in psychology?" Over time, Kelly began to see that she did have some valuable skills, even if she didn't have the ones that were "on the test."

When I started using Spider Web Discussion, I suspected I would see my students improve in the following areas:

- Successful group problem solving and collaboration
- Increased and better participation
- Enhanced communication and social skills
- Improved self-assessment

I did, in fact, see improvement in those areas.

The method is based on group problem solving, so I noticed that students became very adept at working collaboratively in that first year. Through the feedback process, they began to flex and build the muscle of successful group work so that they were taking turns, apologizing for cutting each other off, practicing asking questions more regularly, and valuing the whole group's input. Nowhere to be seen is the perennial classroom problem of "group work," in which one or two students do all the work while the others sit idly by or make half-hearted attempts to help, and then the whole group winds up with the same grade. In footage of a 9th grade classroom discussing *Romeo and Juliet* available on YouTube (Wiggins, 2016), you'll see that by April the students have developed fairly sophisticated group problem-solving (and self-regulating) skills.

As a result of successful collaboration, the next two expected benefits unfold: increased and better participation and enhanced communication and social skills. Because successful group problem solving requires both components, it's only natural that they are strengthened. As you saw in the web graphs of the discussion in Chapter 4, participation evens out and becomes more equal over the first months of using the method, a direct result of enhanced communication and social skills. Students come to understand that talking over others, interruptions, and put-downs lead to poor discussions.

Although I expected improved self-assessment skills, I was still pleased to see that students did, in fact, become quite accurate at this kind of self-assessment. I find that students are quite insightful in assigning themselves a grade, often debating each other to find the perfect-fit value for their discussion. I'm secretly a little pleased when the majority of the group overrides a small minority that always wants to give themselves a top grade, regardless of merit. When this happens, the students who are more accurate will point to the rubric and say things like, "Guys, we didn't do nearly half of these things. Look at the web graph for today at all the interruptions. We can do better." I love when the students take ownership of the assessment in this way.

So I did, in fact, see all the results and benefits I expected to see when I first tried the method. I was also pleasantly surprised to find several unintended benefits that resulted from a classroom culture created around Spider Web Discussion:

- Better assessment data on individual students
- Increase in homework completion
- An ethical and safe classroom environment
- Greater student autonomy
- Opportunities for greater equity

Better Assessment Data

All that coding really pays off. As I mentioned before, when I began to code for students' behavior and contributions alongside the web graph, patterns emerged. In a matter of weeks, I saw that Priyanka had many opinions and loved to contribute but never cited the text to support her ideas; I noticed that Bob nearly always interrupted his classmates; I observed that Julie would contribute rarely but when she did her contributions were usually exceptionally sound, insightful comments or questions that benefited everyone. Having this information on every student gave me a much fuller picture of their strengths and areas of growth and made for much richer parent-teacher conferences, student-teacher conferences, and comments at the end of term. It became very easy for me to say, "Here's what you do well and here are three specific things you can do to improve in this area," and it took almost no effort because the patterns were being tracked during each discussion. I think teachers can use this kind of coding and formative assessment as they see fit. Some will want to dive in and really use it extensively as a way to assess formatively and report. Others are more comfortable with tracking a few key behaviors (such as textual references and interruptions) and focusing on individual behaviors more casually. I don't think there is a formula for how best to use the information. Rather, I think the teacher knows best how she can maximize the data from Spider Web Discussion and use it to her students' advantage. I have played around with various methods over the years depending on the students, class size, total number of students I teach, parent community, and reporting requirements in the schools. I used to track every single behavior in a grade book next to each student's name, which worked fairly easily when I had small class sizes and more autonomous students (as seen in the 9th grade classroom video). Later, I found coding on the web graph sheet enough to give me a big picture and I'd watch as the key patterns developed and make notes in my electronic grade book for me and the student. Most recently, I have focused my coding on key behaviors, such as textual citing, question asking, and depth of analysis, because those skills crossed over into other domains students needed to improve in, such as writing. In this way, I had more pointed suggestions for improvement that related not only to discussions but also to reading analysis and writing. The key takeaway here is that, through the coding, you have more data on your students than you probably need, and it can be insightful for you, students, and parents.

Better Homework Completion

Another unexpected result that many teachers and I have discovered is that students are often perfectly fine with letting their teachers down by not completing assignments or giving their all, but those habits and attitudes can change abruptly when they are letting their peers down. Almost no student wants to be the one who looks bad and brings the group grade down because he didn't complete the reading and can't contribute—even when the grade doesn't "count."

I gave a workshop on SWD to the faculty at a school in Malaysia where I taught. A few days afterward, two of the foreign language teachers approached me, giddy, remarking, "It's amazing, even the slackers do the homework now!" Spider Web Discussion is not a panacea for unmotivated or overstressed students, but it does make class time a lot more relevant for students. They will often come in, asking excitedly, "Are we having a discussion today?" I have never seen students run into class, eyes bright with anticipation, and say, "Are we having a lecture today?" Giving students a voice helps make them autonomous and encourages buy-in. If the homework is designed not as busy work but as a piece of the puzzle that the students must put together during class, then they understand that their part is important and that they have a chance to contribute.

I have had many students over the years say to me with a sly grin, "You know, I never used to read the books until your class. Now I have to."

When I introduce Spider Web Discussion to students, I usually ask them if they have ever seen a real spider web in nature. Nearly all of them say yes. I ask them what happens when you pluck one or two of the strands off the tree or building it's attached to, and a few students reply, "The whole web falls apart."

"Exactly," I say with a smile. "Just like that real spider web in nature, our discussion must involve every single participant anchoring his or her own strand. And what your individual strand might be is going to be different. For some of you, it's speaking up more often because you are afraid to do that. For others, anchoring your strand will be learning to quiet down, listen more, and allow others to get into the conversation more. And for some of you, anchoring your strand might be doing the homework because you let the whole class down when you come unprepared for our discussions. Together, the web is complete when we all pull our own weight and anchor strands. But if even a couple of us don't participate fully, the discussion all falls apart." I find that students understand this visual analogy and take it to heart, and it's a good metaphor to return to periodically as a reminder that all must bring their best to our discussions.

You will have students who do not find your class or the content relevant to their lives and who prefer to focus on other subjects. Some students still skip the readings or don't finish the book, but the truth is I have far fewer than I did before. If you choose texts and essential questions that are meaningful to your students, they'll enjoy having the chance to express their opinions and analysis through a shared, balanced discussion. And they really don't want to let their peers down.

An Ethical and Safe Classroom Environment

When I first started teaching, I naively thought that the best way to teach ethics was to instill in my students a strong set of moral values. I posted artwork and political posters on my classroom walls, forbade the use of derogatory terms related to race, gender, or sexual orientation, and happily schooled my Women's Literature class, especially the wary males, in feminist theory. In short, straight out of college and teaching high school seniors who weren't much younger than me, I thought it was my duty to inculcate these students with my moral beliefs.

The trouble was, it didn't work very well. I wound up alienating more students than I ever reached. Over time, I came to realize that the best way to approach the teaching of ethics is not about teaching the content of ethics but by teaching the process by which the students learn. I began to shift my perception about myself from a teacher who leads her students through the study of ethics to a coach who draws upon the innate ethical talent in her academic athletes. Ethical conduct derives from more than just analysis; the goal is to affect behavior and ultimately produce thoughtful, ethical people. Students should be encouraged not only to examine ethical issues in class but also to experience ethical and unethical conduct directly. Spider Web Discussion provides this opportunity.

When the entire group is rewarded for being engaged and digging deep, students become more aware of their peers and more empathetic. A student who might usually dominate discussion soon learns to ask another student to express her thoughts. A student who interrupts another quickly discovers it's against his and the others' interests, excuses himself, and asks the interrupted student to continue. A student who would never speak if not called upon learns how to speak up during discussions, often surprising the rest of the class with his insights. I've found over the years that when students shift their view of themselves from superstar to a team player, the class dynamic changes radically. Students relax; they bounce ideas off each other; they help each other out; they speak up more or less and they tend to be kinder and more inclusive. Discussions become good because the group, not the individual, is rewarded for it, and nobody wants to bring the rest of the group down—even when it's weighted 0 percent.

Once the students get pretty good at discussions, I encourage *them* to ask good questions more often and remind them that one well-worded and well-timed question can be worth 50 comments. The sharper students pick up on this sooner or later; by the middle of the school year, my classes are asking and answering deep and complicated ethical questions drawn from their texts without any prodding from me. At a school I taught at in Qatar, I found that Ibsen's *Ghosts* came alive and provided hours of riveting discussion on social mores, gossip, and religious hypocrisy—as seen not only through the lens of Ibsen's twentieth-century Norway, but also through that of the students' modern-day Islamic and Arabic culture. Through Spider Web Discussions, students were able to ask the most difficult ethical questions about themselves, their religion, and their culture (a fairly taboo topic there that I would never have broached if leading the discussion myself) and to do so in a thoughtful, productive way.

I'll never forget the 9th grade class I taught in the United States (on which this chapter's vignette is based) in which there was a student, Liam, who was notoriously challenging. He was antisocial and provocative in his statements, and didn't seem to mind if everyone was angry at him or thought him odd. He struggled socially. He was isolated from the class and the dynamic at the start of the year was uncomfortable because he often disagreed with his peers in a way that made them feel less inclined to reach out to him intellectually or personally.

I watched with fascination as Kelly, a popular girl, reached out to him in nearly every discussion. She would turn to him and say kindly, "Liam, what do you think? Do you agree with Sonya or do you feel differently? I'd love to know what your thoughts are." Liam seemed as surprised as I was the first time, but he quickly dove in to a headlong analysis of why Sonya was wrong for one reason or another. But day after day of this dynamic had a curious effect—Kelly's initiative as host paid dividends. Liam saw himself more as a part of the group and everyone softened. Liam's contributions also softened, and everyone seemed a bit captivated by Kelly's empathy. She would often comment after Liam, "That's really insightful. I never saw it that way until you pointed it out." Somehow, just her saying this lifted any clouds over the discussion and you could see others around the table nod in agreement. *It* was *insightful. Thanks, Liam*, they all seemed to think. Kelly's compassion was infectious during Spider Web Discussions and we all benefited from it, thanks to the specific ethical behavior that was able to develop because of the format and norming of the discussions.

Greater Student Autonomy

One of the biggest realizations that I had when I began using Spider Web Discussion was how capable my students were without me. I wasn't really expecting this. For the years prior, I would diligently read my texts and prepare before class, writing out notes and key points that students had to learn. I would use the board to make extensive notes about what was important in a text like *Romeo and Juliet* and expect students to copy them during class. I was the most educated person in the room by anyone's standards, so it seemed only logical that I would be the one determining what was important in a text and highlighting that for students through a combination of lecture, note taking, and discussion that I facilitated in a traditional Socratic way. (I was the Asker of Important Questions.)

When I shifted to the collaborative approach with a group grade and a clear rubric of norms, suddenly I saw that the students didn't need me to point out the key points all the time. In fact, they didn't need me to do it most of the time. I discovered that if I held my tongue for the hour that I allotted for a high school class discussion, the students almost always got to all the points that I wanted them to, and many times to places I hadn't considered. It was very humbling. It made me question what my job really was. With some trepidation, I began to see that my role as resident expert wasn't even that interesting or necessary, especially as Internet search engines and online "cheat sheet" resources were proliferating. If an online resource could tell my students most of the key points in *Romeo and Juliet* before they came to class and heard it from me, then what, really, was my job anyway?

My job became clear as I experimented with silence. I'm by nature a superstar as defined in this book: I love to share my opinion and engage in back-and-forth conversation and, I'm embarrassed to admit, I'm an interrupter. So forcing myself to be the observer was a real learning experience for me. I realized that by being silent and not focusing on my own ideas or knowledge during class discussions allowed me to observe more deeply what students themselves really knew, understood, and could do. It's like being a coach on the sidelines—you can see so clearly how the team is crowding the ball and not spreading out, but it's difficult to see when you are on the playing field. Suddenly, I didn't have the ball. The students had it and they were tasked with passing it to each other as effectively as possible. I was just there as a coach, and viewing my role this way changed my classroom forever. I had more respect for my students and their ideas, and, in turn, I think they developed more respect for me because their voices were given priority over mine during discussion time.

This is not to say that students are running the show or that the teacher has nothing more to offer than being a note taker. A teacher plays a vital role in understanding what constitutes deep learning and transfer and what doesn't, and directing the classroom based on his assessment of those. And a teacher also plays a pivotal role in *training* the students in Spider Web Discussion so that they get good at the process and don't rely on the teacher to direct the discussion, the self-assessment, or the debrief every time. Student autonomy is the goal, and students became more autonomous learners through ethical, inclusive collaboration and self-assessment.

Opportunities for Greater Equity

Equity is a term that has been popping up everywhere in education in the last few years. At its most basic level, equity in education means that students' personal or social circumstances do not impede their opportunity for success. When we have equity in education, factors such as race, gender, socioeconomic status, immigrant status, language ability, disabilities, sexual orientation, and religion do not stand in the way of a student fulfilling her academic potential.

I won't discuss the policy-level research and work being done on equity in education. Rather, I'd like to focus on how Spider Web Discussion can support the movement for equity in education. I have seen it be a vehicle for students from all kinds of backgrounds to deeper learning, a step toward greater equity.

When I present on Spider Web Discussion, teachers who work with low-income student populations, large ELL populations, and special education students sometimes ask if the method is appropriate for their students. The answer is yes. I have personally witnessed student success with all kinds of English language learners over the years. Just as any language teacher would, you may need to adapt the rubric, norms, or pace according to your population's ability and needs, but I have found that the requirement for equal, balanced participation is a great boon to immigrant and ELL students who may otherwise choose to be silent for most of the year. In Spider Web Discussion, they are now asked to be part of the discussion, even if they don't see themselves yet able to discuss as fluently or as quickly as other speakers in the classroom. Whenever there are students with high anxiety or low English ability in my classroom, I make a point to touch base with them one-on-one and provide them some suggestions for how to get into the conversation once or twice in a low-risk way, such as bringing in a question or quote from the text to begin the discussion or using the text to support what others are saying. Dialectical Journals can help a great deal with these students, as their language ability may not be able to keep pace yet with their thinking ability, so having words in front of them can aid in helping get these important voices into the conversation. Getting different, varied, and multicultured voices into the discussion is an important part of equity and we can all benefit from hearing a variety of experiences.

Bettina Meyer, a middle school learning support teacher in an international school, saw SWD modeled by colleagues and was intrigued but noticed that the classes had more than 20 students. She was apprehensive about trying the discussion with her largest class—seven students. Her instructional coach encouraged and gave guidance as Bettina adapted the rubric to her students' needs and set up the first discussion, which was very successful. During that first debrief, a student asked Bettina questions about how often she had spoken and how to improve. This led to Bettina's doing some research online to help the more hesitant students. She found sentence starters (e.g., "I think what I hear you saying is . . . ") and prepared them as a bookmark for her students. Bettina also created a feedback form for each student to use for self-reflection. She was able to copy the individual talk time data from Equity Maps, the iPad app that maps the discussion and tracks student talk time. In the reflections, Bettina asked the students to take data points from Equity Maps and self-evaluate against current and future goals. In this way, Spider Web Discussion became a powerful tool for Bettina's students to set manageable goals and track their communication progress over the course of the year.

Bettina continues to use the method and self-reflection process in her classes, reporting that "all my students love being part of Spider Web Discussion. Not only do I feel it gives each of them a voice, but I love that they can see how they are growing as communicators."

Bettina's colleague Sara Bjork, a middle school ELL teacher, has had a similar experience using Spider Web Discussion in her classes. She was apprehensive about using the method with her small population of English language learners, but when she saw Bettina's success, she wanted to give it a try. Sara liked Bettina's use of goal setting and sentence starters for speaking and listening. Sara asked her students to set some goals before the first discussion that could easily be self-assessed. For example, students picked "I will use five sentence starters" or "I'm going to ask three questions." Additionally, she decided to use Equity Maps to count how many times a student spoke, to track the number of minutes each student spoke, and to track responses based on gender.

Most students were engaged in that first discussion and felt motivated by the Equity Map data because they were able to achieve many goals and identify specific areas of improvement for the next discussion. Sara reports

> Over time, the ELL students have become more comfortable with discussion and each other, and it is very good practice for them to formulate ideas and statements. Further, they take the time to find the right vocabulary to make themselves understood and have now gained the confidence to ask each other for clarifications. They do this because of the norms and because they are patient with each other—something that might not happen in a mainstream class. In our class, they get to try out new vocabulary, sentence starters, and their own ideas while feeling comfortable and secure in the setting.

As we exemplified by the experiences and comments from Bettina and Sara, Spider Web Discussion can be a powerful tool for helping students in ELL or learning support classrooms become confident communicators. You can adapt the method to fit your specific classroom and student needs as long as you stick with the four nonnegotiables of SWD: (1) the students can see one another, face-to-face; (2) the teacher remains silent for the whole discussion time and sits outside the circle; (3) the teacher provides time for students to debrief and self-assess; and (4) the teacher approves or proposes a different grade for the discussion that is criteria-based and collective.

Giving all students a voice and an equal place at the discussion table is not the only way Spider Web Discussion provides opportunities for greater equity. SWD also allows an alternative to writing as a mode in which students can express their knowledge and understanding. Writing is a vital skill. I am not suggesting we reduce our focus on the teaching or importance of writing, but I do believe that we sell short the abilities of many students when we assess their thinking primarily in writing. Writing is a skill that students develop that doesn't necessarily align with students' ability to think. One can be a great writer technically but not a deep, critical thinker; one can be a deep, critical thinker but not a skilled writer. This became apparent to me when I first moved to the Middle East to teach and found the students' writing abilities weaker than those exhibited by my students' in the United States. But these new students had exceptional oral abilities. I was blown away by the conversations the students were having about the literature we read—both the depth and the collaboration were strong—from the very first days. I then discovered that much of Arab-Muslim culture is based on oral tradition and family gatherings involved many hours of discussing and debating. They had highly developed oral expression skills, but most had not been brought up reading or being read to at night, like many U.S. students I had taught. If I had assessed these students only on their writing, I would never have been able to see how deeply they understood the texts we were reading, but I was able to discern their high level of understanding through the use of Spider Web Discussion.

Although we may not always know or understand the social, economic, or cultural factors behind our students' apparent abilities, Spider Web Discussion can help us explore a more complete picture of our students' learning and understanding with greater equity.

What the Research Says

Author Jeremy Rifkin describes how we might develop new teaching models that encourage empathy:

> New teaching models designed to transform education from a competitive contest to a collaborative and empathic learning experience are emerging as schools and colleges try to reach a generation that has grown up on the Internet and is used to interacting in open social networks where information is shared rather than hoarded. (Rifkin, 2010)

The notion that education should be "a collaborative and empathic . . . experience" is valuable and is gaining traction. It resonates with me, as that notion is one of the core goals of Spider Web Discussions and one of the most exciting unintended benefits I have found from the practice. Empathy—and the classroom structures that foster empathy—produce enormous benefits for our students, both in their short-term lives as our students and in their long-term lives as our fellow citizens, colleagues, innovators, and lawmakers.

In addition to increased empathy, you may also find that students become more adept speakers as a result of Spider Web Discussion. In a traditional Socratic seminar that is teacher directed, with the teacher developing and asking the majority of the questions, the students don't get the opportunity to learn to be good question askers the way they do with sustained practice of Spider Web Discussion. As a result, in traditional Socratic seminar, students often spend most of their time listening rather than engaging actively.

Paul Harris, a professor of education at Harvard Graduate School, explores the implications of the frequency of student talk time. He writes that studies show that children ask many more questions at home than they do in school settings. In addition, Harris cites studies that show that teachers greatly underestimate the number of questions they themselves ask, and overestimate the number of questions their students ask in the course of a school day (Harris, 2015). This connects with my own data during teacher observations in the classroom and during Socratic seminars. I will often record teacher talk time versus student talk time during observations and report those numbers on the observation form. For some teachers, particularly those who teach English or social studies, the numbers alone have been eye-opening. Several teachers who spoke a majority of the observation time told me they were bowled over by the data because they had specifically designed lessons in which the students were meant to do the majority of the talking. If we want more student autonomy and critical thinking, we have to shift our thinking about talk time during class. A peer observation or digital recording of your class may help you see how balanced the teacher-to-student talk time is for you and your students.

Because we teachers are usually the ones with the power and knowledge in the classroom, it can be easy to forget what it feels like to be a student. It requires a certain level of empathy to understand how hard it is for students to perform under pressure or how anxious they feel about giving a presentation. I led a workshop on Spider Web Discussion at an international school in Europe in which the participants engaged in a discussion. Afterward, one of the teachers confessed that she realized she was "that" student in her class who was terrified to speak. She noticed her own palms growing sweaty and her heart racing at the thought of having to jump into the conversation with her colleagues. Her experience was quite physical and gave her deep empathy and insight into those students who felt too shy to contribute. She vowed to try a more empathetic, warm approach with them from now on.

Steven Strogatz is a Cornell math professor and author of the book *The Joy of X*. He penned a blog post about a similar experience when he was a student for a day and how it made him feel. He found that he felt uncomfortable when others at his table picked up on things more quickly than he did. In a discussion afterward, he mentioned how embarrassed he was about being the slowest at his table. The experience made him realize how important it was to provide a safe place for his students (Strogatz, 2015).

Empathy is a powerful vehicle to deep learning and understanding. When we understand how someone else feels, we can respond and collaborate more effectively. This is true for teachers, as in Strogatz's case, and true for students in their own collaboration and discussions. Students are capable of facilitating their own insightful, effective, empathic learning environments if we give them the opportunity and guide them through the use of norms and feedback.

I would never argue that students know as much as the teacher or that they can direct the class better than the teacher, but the research supports the notion that if we want to produce graduates who are adept at empathy, inquiry, and collaboration, then we need to give the students ample space and time to hone those skills during our classes each and every day.

Practical Considerations

As you have heard from some of the testimonials and vignettes, a shift toward more student autonomy and greater empathy both to and from the students can be a big change for many teachers. Many of us did not have the kind of relationships with our own teachers that a method like this encourages you to cultivate; it can be hard to change your habits, policies, and comfort levels with social-emotional skills in the classroom.

So the first practical consideration is to think through the relationships that you have with your students and the relationships they have with one another. What are the barriers to creating greater empathy and autonomy? What can you do in the short term to reduce the barriers? In the long term? Don't think you need to dive off the high dive on the first day if neither you nor your students feel emotionally ready. Feel free to wade in gently, testing the waters a bit with regard to how often, how long, and how experimental Spider Web Discussion is for you. You might try a brief discussion on an engaging text once this month, and, if it goes well, you can build several discussions into an upcoming unit where they will fit nicely with the planned topics. I find that in a high school English class that meets every day, two to three times a week seems to be just the right frequency. For elementary students, a brief daily discussion during reading instruction might be appropriate for a whole unit or you might prefer a weekly approach to discuss key readings, concepts, or problems in the core subjects.

The discussion frequency also depends on the type of unit we are doing. If we are working on writing and performance, there may be less room for Spider Web Discussion on a daily or weekly basis than if we were reading a book together and want to analyze and discuss it. Given your schedule, curriculum, and class time, you should find the pattern that works best for you and your students.

Another practical consideration is deciding when to redirect the discussion if students get way off topic, if they go down a path of misinformation, or if they say things that are just plain wrong. You will also have to decide when to redirect if they (intentionally or not) say things that could be highly offensive or hurtful to others in the room, specifically related to topics that touch on race, class, religion, gender, or sexual orientation.

When the students are just going down a path of misinformed or flat-out-wrong inquiry, I tend to wait longer than I am comfortable with to see if someone in the group rights the wrong. More often than not, if I wait those first few minutes, other students will correct the students who misunderstood. I make a point to encourage that student behavior during the debriefing process. I think it's a crucial life skill to learn how to question, evaluate, and correct others in group work. When my students don't self-correct as a group after a few minutes and I see that their misunderstanding is leading to counterproductive exploration, I will briefly correct a factual error or suggest a closer look at the passage and then return to quietly observing and taking notes again. I try to be as unobtrusive as possible so that I remain the coach and not the judge or star player in these circumstances. I want them to know that the goal is autonomy; eventually, they should learn to correct their own errors in thinking and reading.

If there are potentially hurtful or offensive comments during SWD, I urge you to proceed with caution depending on your student population and curriculum. I strongly feel that all teachers should engage in equity and social justice training when possible. The one-week summer training I attended at Phillips Exeter's Diversity Institute changed my thinking about equity in the classroom forever, and I will always be grateful to their faculty for opening my eyes to ways in which I may not have understood many marginalized students' experiences. I found that it's possible to be a thoughtful, open-minded, well-intentioned teacher who values diverse perspectives and yet unconsciously create a classroom environment where some students feel uncomfortable. If we are studying or discussing a text that has the potential to trigger discomfort, pain, or past trauma, I try to pay special attention to the norming process before and during these discussions and topics. I will perhaps talk more openly in the classroom about what needs to happen in order for everyone to feel safe enough that they can learn to their highest potential. I also solicit anonymous feedback more regularly with regard to specific feelings about the topic and the challenges it poses. A discussion of a text like Mark Twain's *Huck Finn* can be a powder keg for students who don't have the language tools, intercultural experience, or social context to handle racial discussions with adequate sensitivity; it requires careful planning, established trust, and empathy to navigate these discussions.

When you are weighing the balance between important learning on social and political topics and maintaining a trusting, productive classroom environment, I recommend a few things. First, don't start the year with the most challenging, sensitive topics, as they are best and most deeply explored later in the year when norms and trust are established. Second, you may find yourself needing to intervene more often to avoid or reduce (unintentional) hurtful comments, such as one student putting another on the spot to speak about how it feels to be the black/immigrant/gay/wealthy/ELL kid. Third, you might find that your students do not have the level of trust or maturity yet to deal with these complex issues productively, so choose more appropriate texts or guide them a bit more during discussions so they can model a more thoughtful, respectful approach.

At the end of the day, Spider Web Discussion usually leads to more ethical, empathetic approaches to any text that you might explore as a class, but *when in doubt, choose kindness.* Sometimes choosing kindness means stepping in a bit more than usual to ensure that all students are protected from potential bigotry with regard to a particularly sensitive topic. It doesn't mean the students shouldn't grapple with difficult issues on their own. It just means you might need to be more referee and team captain than coach at these times in the interest of creating safe, productive learning spaces.

Advanced Applications

One of the best and most eye-opening professional development experiences I have ever had is filming my teaching and watching it. I strongly suggest that you film yourself on a regular teaching day (prior to doing your first Spider Web Discussion) and watch it. Note everything that stands out to you. Consider student behavior, engagement, seating arrangements, and teacher/student talk time. In addition, ask a trusted colleague to come in and observe you on a regular teaching day and track the student/teacher talk time and give you feedback targeted to some specific goals you want to achieve during the class (e.g., increased student questioning).

Once you have reviewed this feedback, design backward from what you want to see happen in your first Spider Web Discussion. If you noticed with surprise how much you talked, make it a goal to not speak during the upcoming discussion and stick to it. If you find that students lacked engagement at certain moments when you were giving instructions, aim to give only brief instructions for the first Spider Web Discussion to see if they seem more responsive. During the first discussion, track the teacher and student talk time again and note the changes later with that same colleague or even with your students. What differences did you feel between the two lessons? How about your students?

School leaders might also consider how they can use Spider Web Discussion for faculty meetings or professional development. How might using Equity Maps, an app for diagramming conversations, illuminate dynamics with regard to talk time during faculty meetings? How might faculty engaging in the method themselves through a half-hour discussion on a gripping read or short film, using the norms, offer a unique professional growth experience? How might dedicated, experienced practitioners on the faculty invite parents to try the method in an effort to educate them on the skills their children are honing in class? There are advanced applications for the use of the method with the adults in the community as well as the students.

Voices from the Field

—RAYYAN AMINE, PHD, 8TH GRADE MATH TEACHER, FORMER ASSISTANT SUPERINTENDENT FOR SCHOOL IMPROVEMENT IN CYPRESS-FAIRBANKS INDEPENDENT SCHOOL DISTRICT, HOUSTON, TX—I first heard of the Spider Web Discussion method from my daughter who uses it in her 10th grade English class. I was intrigued by the concept and by her excitement. I then had the opportunity to attend a session taught by Alexis that got me more interested. I was determined to try it with my 8th grade math class. The search began for an appropriate topic to introduce SWD to my six math periods—and my middle school learning coach found the perfect one. The video was about math mindsets, a topic that I have been wanting to discuss with my 8th graders to highlight the importance of math and looking at the subject as useful and meaningful rather than something difficult some students were just not meant for. Alexis facilitated the first two class periods while I observed; I continued with the remaining four.

My first takeaway was the rich discussion that the Spider Web Discussion process promoted. I admit that I went into this activity thinking that I was doing something meaningful for the students; however, it ended up being an enriching learning experience for me. For the first time I heard my students talk about math and what they like and dislike about it, what they fear and what they love, and the way they would like it to be taught. They articulated their ideas and drew various connections with other content areas to explain how math can become more approachable for them. Another takeaway was the one I noticed after the introductory sessions: I could sense different dynamics in my classes. My students seemed more comfortable in math class, as if this process had fostered a greater sense of safety and had given them a green light to feel more empathetic toward one another. The rubric that Alexis shared included items such as "taking risks" and "sharing opinions." Although these ideas were not new to my students, seeing them on a rubric almost walked the walk of how important they were.

After teaching the students for one full term, I found that the ones who were the least engaged in math class all of a sudden had become the most engaged in the Spider Web Discussion—a surprising but welcome phenomenon. Students were confident and assertive and had remarkably interesting comments. The discussions were rich and the engagement was exceptionally high, especially among the students who rarely participated in math class. It felt as if the Spider Web Discussion process gave them a perfect opportunity to express themselves. My students in all periods quickly understood the process, they embraced it and purposefully tried to engage others and include everyone in the conversation—something that they had not necessarily done in regular classes.

I plan to continue to look for ways to include the process more frequently in my class. I believe the inclusion of such a process is innovative and aligned with the 21st century skills that we wish for our students to develop, such as the ability to communicate clearly, collaborate, take responsibility for their learning, and set their trajectory to becoming life-long learners.

Big Takeaway

I have seen many benefits over the decade I have been using and sharing Spider Web Discussion; some are obvious and expected, and others have surprised me and other teachers using the method. Most of the research highlighted throughout this book points to a world in which we need highly skilled, empathetic, collaborative problem solvers, and Spider Web Discussion offers students and teachers a chance to develop these skills.

An administrator at an international school who had asked me to train faculty in Spider Web Discussion confessed that she had been using Spider Web Discussion for years and was amazed at the high-level discussion and well-mannered behavior of her 6th grade students during class time. But then she would walk into a faculty meeting and see her colleagues talking over one another, interrupting, using body language or making comments that might be off-putting to some—all behaviors the rubric asks students to avoid—and she would think to herself: *Wow, my 6th graders are better at this than we are!*

The goal of Spider Web Discussion is to help students—and educators—develop lifelong skills that benefit us as individuals and as a society. With sustained practice of the method in your classroom, you can create a culture in which collaboration, empathy, autonomy, and equity are within everyone's reach.

8 LOOKING AHEAD: A YEAR OF SPIDER WEB DISCUSSION

When Chris started using Spider Web Discussion in his first year of teaching at a new school, it was a lonely exercise and an uphill battle. Although he was seeing good success with it in his own classroom and was pleased with the results, he found that his colleagues weren't interested in trying the approach and some of the parents and administrators questioned this method in which the teacher "wasn't teaching." He had a handful of tense conversations that year with parents and his principal about the purpose of the method. He explained that it was a highly designed, structured method that led to deeper inquiry and greater collaboration and participation; it was not "students running the show."

In his second year at the school, though, a new colleague heard about what Chris was doing and asked to observe him. Imani was really impressed with the results he was getting—high-level inquiry, greater student independence, and more engagement—and she wanted to try it as well. Imani asked Chris to coach her in the first few weeks and months, which led to a long-term collaborative friendship. Together, they approached the principal and asked if they could present the method and their data to the rest of the faculty. They wanted to share their success with others. The principal, despite his initial hesitation the year before, was convinced by the pair's enthusiasm and gave them the OK.

Many faculty members responded positively to Chris's and Imani's presentation, which included video footage of deep discussions by students not always known for their insightful contributions. The rest of the English department and the history department wanted to give Spider Web Discussion a try based on the video footage and data they had seen. A few science teachers and even a math teacher were also intrigued and followed up with Chris and Imani, asking them for copies of the rubric and some advice on how to get started.

Two years later, the language of Spider Web Discussion, the web graphing, the group grading, and the self-assessment were something all students and most of the faculty in the school were familiar with. The method became easier to use as more teachers used it because the students already knew what it was and how to do it. Teachers no longer had to train students in the basics nor "sell" them on the idea. Teachers were pleased to find that they were spending less time going over the mechanics beforehand and less time debriefing the process, because students were already skilled at it. Having a common language and shared experience across much of the school raised everyone's game. Chris never had to have tense conversations about the method anymore; instead, he enjoyed helping students take their discussions to the next level and helping colleagues with the occasional question. It had become a schoolwide ethos, no longer an uphill battle he was fighting alone.

When I began to present on Spider Web Discussion, workshop attendees asked for a short instruction manual on how to begin, so I created one. You'll find a brief, step-by-step set of instructions below, which explains how to begin with Spider Web Discussion from the first day and continue with it throughout the year.

A Year of Spider Web Discussion

1. Put the desks or students in an oval or circle (or two circles if you have more than 24 students). Everyone should be able to see everyone else clearly from their seats.
2. Show a "model" Spider Web Discussion, either in video footage or by modeling it with other teachers or students, and ask for the students' reactions.

3. Pass out your tailor-made rubric, and sit down with the students at the table to discuss it. Note especially the whole class assessment and discuss their reaction to this factor.

4. Assign a reading, essential question, problem, or short film that they will use to prepare for or watch for the first discussion. Make it as kid-friendly and engaging as possible. I often use "Fake Empire" (Lewis, 2009) or "How They Get There" (Landay & Jonze, 1997). I usually take this time to draw the map of the students' names while they watch so I have it ready to go.

5. Set an age-appropriate amount of time. For 8th or 9th grade students, I start the first discussion with 30 minutes; 40 minutes for older students. For upper-elementary students in grades 6 and 7, try from 20 to 25 minutes. For the littlest students, 10 minutes is a good time to start with.

6. Make sure you have your "web" (circle) of names ready before the students begin.

7. Sit in the back of the room in a chair or student desk—not at your own desk, which connotes power—and take notes while they run the discussion until the time is up.

8. Do not save them from silence. Don't interrupt or correct them. Let them learn that you won't help them in this endeavor—they will need to help themselves.

9. For elementary school students, scaffold quite a bit (perhaps assign roles or use smaller groups).

10. As the students discuss the assigned work, draw the "web" of the conversation. Don't tell them what you are doing while you do this. Just let them think you're taking notes.

11. Code for a few key actions the first time, especially "I" for interruptions, "T" for text references, "Ad" for advancing the conversation. This is good feedback for them to hear at the end of the discussion.

12. When the time is up, share the web with them (preferably via overhead or interactive whiteboard, if you can). Students love to see it. Let them make sense of it first by commenting, laughing, asking questions before you explain it. They love to ask "What is 'I?'" and they usually laugh when you explain that it means "interruptions."

13. Sit down with them at their circle, preferably in the same type of seat they have. Ask the students to self-assess in pairs against the rubric and come up with a letter grade for the discussion based on the criteria. Assure them that today is only a practice grade.

14. Debrief the discussion's *process* first—who spoke a lot, who didn't get into the conversation yet. Discuss whether interruptions are a problem; if they are, discuss them without judgment of those who interrupt but kindly encourage those students to work on avoiding interruptions next time. A great question to keep the focus on students' independence at this stage is to ask: "According to the rubric, what did we do well today?" and follow it up with, "What can we do better next time?"

15. Discuss the grades the pairs came up with and come to a consensus as a group, taking into account your feedback as the observer.

16. Next, spend 10–15 minutes debriefing the actual discussion *content* and what insightful remarks or questions were shared and ways you hoped the students would build on them but didn't yet. This is the place to play your traditional teacher role where you redirect the conversation to anywhere it didn't go deeply enough or probe students further. But do so staying seated at the table with them to avoid a power imbalance.

17. Ask them if they'd like to try the method again. If the majority say yes, encourage them to do better. If the majority say no, find out specifically why not and see if you can address their concerns so that they are willing to keep trying.

18. Keep a clipboard or database of discussion webs (I date them, put the self-assessed grade on them, and jot down a bit of feedback to summarize each one). Keep the clipboard or database accessible in your classroom or online so students can track their progress over the year.

19. With the second discussion, reiterate the criteria and ask students to recall the specific improvement goals. Repeat the discussion process again, perhaps allowing longer on the clock this time as you see fit.

20. Debrief after this discussion and every subsequent discussion. Always allow enough time to show them the web graphs, ask students to self-assess against the rubric, and solicit and provide feedback. Tell them how to do better each time ("These people are having trouble speaking

up—why don't you each bring in a question next time and ask your question? These people are interrupting a lot. No one is referring to the text much, so that will be a main goal for next time.")

21. When they are more comfortable with SWD, have students take turns doing the web on the clipboard and doing simple codes ("I" for interruptions and "Q" for questions) themselves. Many students really like to do this. Students (grade 10 and below) struggle to map and participate a lot at the same time, so I allow them to speak less or not at all when they map. Students in grades 11–12 can do both without much trouble.

22. Celebrate the milestones and improvements (the first Bs and As; the first time a shy student spoke without being prompted).

23. Throughout the year, and especially at the end, spend some time showing them their progress by flipping through the webs and asking them to self-assess their individual and class growth in Spider Web Discussion. Always remember the "P" in Spider: it's a *process*.

24. Don't be afraid to ask for anonymous feedback via Survey Monkey or other apps that don't require handwriting to find out how the students feel about the method throughout the year. Like Beth in the testimonial in Chapter 5, don't be deterred by initial resistance or get upset. Instead, use the feedback at regular intervals to track patterns and growth over the course of the year. The feedback from a year's worth of use can paint a more positive picture than the first snapshot, especially if this is a very new or unusual way of learning for students.

Practical Considerations

Like Chris in this chapter's opening vignette, being the only teacher in your school using Spider Web Discussion can sometimes feel challenging or lonely. You might want to enlist an ally in your department or division to try it with you for coaching, advice, and moral support. It can be hard to carry out if you feel you are the only one in the school interested or willing to try the method, and it can be doubly hard if you don't have support within your team, department, or division.

Spider Web Discussion is good in a classroom, great across several disciplines, and fantastic schoolwide. Enlist critical friends, allies, and coaches who can engage in the method with you and give you feedback as you go so that you and your students are not working in isolation.

Advanced Applications

I've had positive experiences asking students to reflect on their learning twice a year, generally at the end of each term. I ask them to pull out portfolios of their written work, their rubrics, and their feedback over the term and ask them to note, in writing, how they feel they have grown and what they think they have gained as a learner. I ask them to compare their first writing assignment of the year with the most recent one and make specific comparisons and contrasts, demystifying the assessment and growth process for them and giving them a sense of accomplishment.

I also recommend doing this for Spider Web Discussion. As part of that same reflection, have students compare the first couple web graphs of the year with the most recent ones, asking students to reflect on their collaborative and individual growth over the course of the term with regard to discussions. These written reflections also make great fodder for student comments and parent-teacher conferences. Self-reflections in the students' own words carry a lot of weight for parents.

If your goal is to enlist more interested teachers, share a video highlighting the method, such as the one of my 9th grade English class (Wiggins, 2016), in a faculty meeting or during a professional development day and discuss teachers' reactions and ideas. You can follow up with articles to read and discuss, such as the ones I have cited throughout the book that support the need for better teaching and assessing of collaboration, empathy, and student autonomy.

Voices from the Field

—CRYSTAL VAN CLEEF, MIDDLE SCHOOL HUMANITIES TEACHER FROM CLEARWATER, FL—Throughout my teaching career, I'd heard of a wide variety of teaching strategies and discussion techniques; however, student-led discussions was one that I kept consistently hearing about. Teachers that I respected and aspired to be like would often use that type of discussion in their classes and I was intrigued but apprehensive about trying it myself, especially since these teachers were almost always high school teachers and I was a middle school teacher. Although the idea of student-led discussions sounded like the perfect way to truly give ownership of their learning to my students, logistically I was clueless how to do it and I knew that if I didn't do it well, it could easily go downhill quickly. So the years passed and I never gave it a try, until this year.

The learning coach in my division told me about the Spider Web Discussion method that Alexis had introduced to our high school with great success, and she suggested that it might be worth trying in one of my classes. Although I was very interested, again I was a bit skeptical of how well it would work in the middle school, especially with my 6th grade students. Alexis was eager to take on my 6th graders and confident it would work, and boy was she right! They rose to the occasion and far exceeded my expectations, which was exciting to witness. The Spider Web Discussion laid out the logistics for me and my students clearly, which provided the structure necessary for success.

After seeing the success with my 6th graders, I knew I had to try it out on my own with my 8th grade classes. Before my first class started, I felt a mixture of anxiety and nervous excitement, because I wasn't sure if what I saw with my other class was just due to Alexis's expertise—she had introduced them to the method for that first great discussion. I discovered quickly, though, that even in 8th grade and without the "expert" in the room, the students were still just as eager to take responsibility for their own learning. In fact, many seemed to crave the freedom to express themselves openly in a way this method allows. Students who usually sit passive in class were suddenly attentive and contributing to the class discussion. I don't know if I've felt as proud of my students as I did when I saw them making connections, thinking in depth, and truly listening to each other.

You don't need an expert in the room—just the courage to try it.

Overall Takeaway

Crystal's testimonial beautifully sums up what many teachers around the world have discovered: just give Spider Web Discussion a shot and you will likely be very pleased by the results. You don't need an expert to run the discussion; all you need is a little courage to try something new. Although you are welcome to attend one of my Spider Web Discussion institutes any time you'd like more training or insights into the method, it isn't necessary. Any teacher with a good rubric, a piece of paper, and a pencil can begin Spider Webbing tomorrow.

When I present on Spider Web Discussions in schools and at conferences, I remind the audience that SWD is not an activity, it's a classroom philosophy. Although it can be used as an occasional activity, its power is found in a sustained practice that builds a culture of shared inquiry over time, through feedback and self-assessment. I also like to remind audience members that if the method doesn't resonate with you, don't use it. I'm not trying to sell a product or convert people to a certain style of teaching. I wrote this book and speak with teachers around the world on the topic because I am such a firm believer in the ability of Spider Web Discussion to empower students to be top-notch thinkers and collaborators. In all my years of teaching, this is the one tool in my toolbox that has been the most effective, hands down. I want to share it with as many interested educators as possible because I think that the more we can teach students to own their learning and inquiry, the stronger education becomes overall. Spider Web Discussion is the way I have discovered how to do this most effectively in my classroom.

One day, early on in my teaching at the Masters School, where I was first introduced to the Harkness style of teaching, a colleague was joking about how empowering high-level, student-run discussions could be.

> I had to miss a day of class to attend a conference in the city. That morning, I set up a camera on a tripod in the corner of the classroom and I left instructions with the students to have a Harkness discussion. Later, when I came back from the conference and watched the tape, I was surprised and a little taken aback to note it was the best class I'd ever taught!

To me, this epitomizes what school should be about. We talk about words like autonomy, transfer, and lifelong learning, but how often do we get students to really practice or achieve them? Why not give students an opportunity to take the content they have been grappling with, apply the skills of critical thinking, collaboration, communication, and empathy, and produce something truly unique—a deep inquiry that is entirely student led? This is the living definition of transfer.

I invite you to try Spider Web Discussion, regardless of what age or subject you teach. Find or create a rubric that works for you, assign a text, question, or problem, explain the parameters and goals, set aside an age-appropriate amount of time, and then sit back and observe. I think you'll be surprised.

It may just be the best class you never taught.

REFERENCES

Anders, G. (2005, August 17). That useless liberal arts degree has become tech's hottest ticket. *Forbes*. Retrieved from https://www.forbes.com/sites/georgeanders/2015/07/29/liberal-arts-degree-tech/

Bajak, A. (2014, May 12). Lectures aren't just boring. They're ineffective, too, study finds. *Science*. Retrieved from http://www.sciencemag.org/news/2014/05/lectures-arent-just-boring-theyre-ineffective-too-study-finds

Brennan, E. (2013, July 21). A pilot's views on flight safety. *New York Times*, p. TR3.

Briggs, S. (2014, November 1). How empathy affects learning and how to cultivate it in your students. *informED*. Retrieved from http://www.opencolleges.edu.au/informed/features/empathy-and-learning/

Bryant, A. (2011, March 13). The quest to build a better boss. *New York Times*, p. BU1.

Dahl, M. (2016, March 18). How schools are failing their quietest students. *Science of Us*. Retrieved from http://nymag.com/scienceofus/2016/03/how-schools-are-failing-their-quietest-students.html

Deming, D. J. (2015). The growing importance of social skills in the labor market. *Working Paper Series, 21473*. Stanford, CA: National Bureau of Economic Research.

Dewey, J. (1916/2009). *Democracy and education: An introduction to the philosophy of education*. Waiheke Island: Floating Press.

Duhigg, C. (2016, February 28). What Google learned from its quest to build the perfect team. *New York Times*, p. MM20.

Feger, M. (2006). 'I want to read': How culturally relevant texts increase student engagement in reading. *Multicultural Education, 13*(3), 18–19.

Friedman, T. (2014, February 22). How to get a job at Google. *New York Times*, p. SR11. Retrieved from https://www.nytimes.com/2014/02/23/opinion/sunday/friedman-how-to-get-a-job-at-google.html

Gaudet, A. D., Ramer, L. M., Nakonechny, J., Cragg, J. J., Ramer, M. S., & Fuller, D. Q. (2010). Small-group learning in an upper-level university biology class enhances academic performance and student attitudes toward group work. *PLOS ONE, 5*(12).

Goldring, R., Gray, L., & Bitterman, A. (2013). *Characteristics of public and private elementary and secondary school teachers in the United States: Results from the 2011–12 schools and staffing survey* (NCES 2013-314). U.S. Department of Education. Washington, DC: National Center for Education Statistics. Retrieved December 19, 2016 from http://nces.ed.gov/pubsearch.

Harris, P. (2015, September). What children learn from questioning. *Educational Leadership, 73*(1), 28–29.

Kuhn, D. (2015, January). Thinking together and alone. *Educational Researcher, 44*(1), 46–53.

Landay, V. (Producer), and Jonze, S. (Director). (1997). "How they get there" [Video file]. United States: Palm Pictures.

Lewis, R. (Producer). (2009, September 25). "Ryan Lewis—fake empire" [Video file]. Retrieved from https://www.youtube.com/watch?v=MdoliLNRlHo

Mazur, E. [Derek Bok Center, Harvard University]. (2013a, November 19). *Assessment: The silent killer of learning.* [Video file]. Retrieved from https://www.youtube.com/watch?v=CBzn9RAJG6Q&t=121s

Mazur, E. [HarvardEducation]. (2013b, November 14). *Masterclass with Eric Mazur: Confessions of a converted lecturer.* [Video file]. Retrieved from https://www.youtube.com/watch?v=863iYozllxE

McTighe, J., & Wiggins, G. (2013). *Essential questions: Opening doors to student understanding.* Alexandria, VA: ASCD.

Miller, C. C. (2015, October 16). Why what you learned in preschool is crucial at work. *New York Times*, p. SR4.

National Center for Education Statistics. (2017, May). Racial/ethnic enrollment in public schools. *The Condition of Education.* Retrieved from https://nces.ed.gov/programs/coe/indicator_cge.asp

National Governors Association Center for Best Practices & Council of Chief State School Officers. (2010). *Common Core State Standards.* Washington, DC: Authors.

Patterson, R. E., III. (2012). *The role of culturally relevant texts and comprehension strategy instruction in the literacy engagement of African American adolescent males.* (Doctoral dissertation). University of Pittsburgh.

Pink, D. (2009). *Drive: The surprising truth about what motivates us.* New York: Riverhead Books.

Rifkin, J. (2010, May 30). Empathic education: The transformation of learning in an interconnected world. *The Chronicle of Higher Education.* Available: www.chronicle.com/article/empathic-education-the/65695.

Smith, M. K., Wood, W. B., Adams, W. K., Wieman, C., Knight, J. K., Guild, N., & Su, T. T. (2009, January). Why peer discussion improves student performance on in-class concept questions. *Science, 323*(5910), 122–124.

Smith, M. K., Wood, W. B., Krauter, K., & Knight, J. K. (2011, March). Combining peer discussion with instructor explanation increases student learning from in-class concept questions. *Life Sciences Education, 10*(1), 55–63.

Strauss, V. (2014, October 14). Teacher spends two days as a student and is shocked by what she learns [blog post]. Retrieved from *The Answer Sheet* at https://www.washingtonpost.com/news/answer-sheet/wp/2014/10/24/teacher-spends-two-days-as-a-student-and-is-shocked-at-what-she-learned/?utm_term=.2f4409039560.

Strogatz, S. (2015, June 12). Teaching through inquiry: A beginner's reflections [blog post]. Retrieved from *Discovering the Art of Mathematics* at https://www.artofmathematics.org/blogs/cvonrenesse/steven-strogatz-reflection-part-1.

Thompson, M. (2004). Why are we afraid of our boys? A psychologist looks at solutions. *Children & Libraries: The Journal of the Association for Library Service to Children, 2*(1), 26–30.

Tilsley, A. (2013, January 18). Advanced placement, not credit. *Inside Higher Ed.* Retrieved from https://www.insidehighered.com/news/2013/01/18/dartmouth-end-use-advanced-placement-scores-credit.

Trustees of Phillips Exeter Academy. (2017). The Harkness gift. *Phillips Exeter Academy.* Retrieved from https://www.exeter.edu/about-us/harkness-gift.

Wiggins, A. (2014, March 29). Q&A discussion-based learning math. *Alexis Wiggins's Wiki.* Retrieved December 20, 2016 from http://alexiswiggins.pbworks.com/w/file/59054896/Q%26ADiscussionBasedLearningMath.docx.

Wiggins, A. (2016, July 21). *Alexis Wiggins-spider web discussion-grade 9 ELA.* [Video File]. Retrieved from https://www.youtube.com/watch?v=jHi06vm5uJk.

Wiggins, G. (2012, October). *International baccalaureate address.* [Video File]. Retrieved from vimeo.com/iboorg/review/53933572/ac28bd7357.

INDEX

The letter *f* following a page number denotes a figure.

apps for SWD graphs, 124
assessment. *see also* group grades
    AP exams, 54
    equitable, 142
    peer discussion during, 56
    practical considerations, 121
    self-assessment, student, 29, 49, 131–132
assessment data, 133–134
autonomy, 134, 137–138

caring, 119–120
classes, large, 63–66
class periods, short, 63–64
classroom setup, 26
coding, 27, 36–37, 38*f*, 39–40, 133
collaboration
    as benefit of SWD, 131–132
    peer discussion for learning physics,
      50–54
    in the rubric, 21–22
    workplace, 4, 11, 14
college and career readiness standard, 12
Common Core State Standards (CCSS)
    English-Language Arts, 12, 125–126
    Mathematics, 126–127
communication skills, 11, 131–132
community-based discussion culture, 25–26
control, relinquishing, 17, 41–42

debriefing
    first day, 28-31
    first few weeks, 48–50
    nonnegotiables, 31*f*

Dialectical Journals (DJs), 86–87, 86*f*, 87*f*, 89*f*, 89*f*,
    90, 139
discussion, allotting time for, 24–28, 48
discussion bullies, 69–70
diversity, student, 102–103

empathy, 34, 97–99, 120, 130–131, 136–137, 142–144
engagement, 102–103, 118, 128
English-Language Arts
    CCSS for, 12, 125–126
    SWD in middle school, 58
English language learners, 139–141
equity, 102–103, 138–139, 145
Equity Maps, 124
ethical environment, 135–137
extroverts, 80–81

feedback
    anonymous, 145
    coding for, 39–40
    first few weeks, 49–50
    group grades for, 115–113, 120, 122
    the web for, 28
    workplace, 11
feedback giver role, 95, 107
formative assessment, group grades in, 7, 13

Google, 10–11, 33–34
grades. *see also* group grades
    incentive-performance link, 121
    participation, 68–69, 113–114
    recording, 123–124
    as weapons, 116, 122

graphs, SWD
    apps for, 124
    assessment data from, 133–134
    drawing, 27
    feedback from, 123–124
    first day examples, 71f, 76f
    participation balance, increasing, 73f, 74f,
        77f, 78f, 79f
    web grapher role, 106
group grades
    benefits, 7
    counting, 7–8, 113–117
    as feedback mechanism, 115–116, 120, 122
    first day, 26, 29
    first few weeks, 48–49
    nonnegotiables, 31f
    practical considerations, 13, 121, 122–123
    in the rubric, 21
    vignette, 111–112
group problem solving, 131–132

Harkness method, 6–8, 45–47
higher education skills, 14–15
homework completion, 134–135
host, role of, 95–96, 106

incentive-performance link, 121
inclusion, 34
interruptions, 75–77, 76f, 77f, 79
introverts, 80–81

key passage leader role, 106
kindness, 119–120, 123, 145–146

learning, peer discussion and, 50–54
listening, 72
literary terms leader role, 107
low-income students, 139

managers, traits of good, 10–11
math
    CCSS for, 126–127
    SWD in, 43–47, 60–63, 147–148
motivation, 115–116, 118, 121–122
multimedia texts, 22–23

norming, 33–35

participation
    creating balance in, 70–77, 73f, 74f, 78f, 79–81,
        79f
    effective, meaning of, 69
    grading, 68–69, 112–114
    increasing, 75, 131–132

peer discussion, learning and, 50–54
Peer Instruction model, 56
physics, peer discussion to learn, 50–54
power dynamic, student-teacher, 117–119, 128
Project Oxygen (Google), 10–11

Quiet Schools Movement, 80–81

relationships, student-teacher, 118–119, 144,
    145–146
relevance, importance of, 22–24, 134
roles, assigning, 105–107
rubric
    collaboration in the, 21–22
    designing the, 17, 19, 21–22, 33
    elementary rubric, 19f
    English-Language Arts, 18f
    group grades in the, 21
    introducing the, 25–26
    norms, 33–35
    Spanish 19, 20f
    successful, 33–35
rubric leader role, 106

safe spaces, 34, 85, 104–105, 128, 135–137, 145
science, SWD in, 55–57
screens, turning off, 25–26
self-assessment, student, 29, 48, 131–132
self-regulating skills, 132
silence, 27–28, 72–73, 137–138
social sensitivity, 34
social skills, 3–4, 10, 10–11, 34, 54–55, 130–132,
    131–132. see also empathy
social studies, SWD in second grade, 59–60
soft skills. see social skills
speaking skills, 142
special education students, 139
Spider Web Discussion (SWD)
    challenging situations, strategies for,
        104–105, 110
    coding, 27, 36–37, 38f, 39–40, 133–134
    components, 9
    the first few weeks, 47–50
    frequency of, 144
    goal of, 5, 9, 149
    group self-correction, 145
    history of, 6–9
    hurtful comments during, 145–146
    ideal number of students, 63
    interruptions, 75–77, 76f, 77f, 79
    introduction to, 5
    journaling prior to, 86–87, 86f, 87f, 88f, 89f,
        90
    in large classes, 63–66

Spider Web Discussion (SWD) (*continued*)
  nonnegotiables, 31*f*, 141
  offensive comments during, 145
  participation, balancing, 70–77, 73*f*, 74*f*, 78*f*, 79, 79*f*
  redirecting the, 144–145
  reflection prior to, 85
  research findings, 31–35, 50–55, 80–82, 143–144
  roles, assigning, 95, 105–107
  sensitive topics, 146
  silence during, 27–28, 72–73
  successful, the rubric in, 33–35
Spider Web Discussion (SWD) benefits
  assessment data, 133–134
  autonomy, 137–138
  collaboration, 131–132
  communication skills, 131–132
  to ELL students, 139–141
  empathy, 142
  equity, 138–139
  group problem solving, 131–132
  homework completion, 134–133
  participation, increased, 131–132
  self-assessment, 131–132
  self-regulating skills, 132
  social skills, 131–132
  speaking skills, 142
Spider Web Discussion (SWD) first day
  advice from the field, 127
  coding student behavior, 27
  considerations prior to, 35
  debriefing, 28–31
  drawing the web, 27
  failure on, 71, 71*f*
  the group grade, 26, 29
  helpful colleagues, 35
  the introduction, 24–25, 30
  nonnegotiables, 35
  room setup, 26
  the rubric, introducing, 25–26
  screens, turning off, 25–26
  silence, managing, 27–28
  student self-assessment, 29
  the teacher's role, 24–28
  text, choosing the, 22–24
  time for discussion, allotting, 24–28
  topic, choosing the, 22–24, 146
  vignette, 111–112

Spider Web Discussion (SWD) implementation
  considerations prior to, 12–14, 121, 146–147
  designing the rubric, 17, 18*f*, 19, 19*f*, 20*f*, 21–22
  vignette, 150–151, 155–156
  a year of steps for, 151–154
Spider Web Discussion Key, 38*f*
statistics, SWD in high school, 60–63
students
  bad behavior–personal problem link, 99–100
  boys, 101–102
  bright, talkative (superstar), 68–72, 75–77, 79–83, 94–96
  challenging/defiant, 93–99, 102, 110, 119–120, 130–131, 136–137
  emotional lives of, attending to, 99–101
  as partners, 117–118
  response to SWD, 47–48, 67–68, 107–109
  role in SWD, 9
  self-assessment, 29, 48, 131–132
  self-regulating skills, 132
  shy, reticent, quiet, 68–72, 80–81, 83–85, 91, 95–96
student-teacher power dynamic, 117–118, 144

teachers
  control, relinquishing, 17, 41–42
  demographics, 102–103
  power of, 117–119, 128
  role as expert, 137–138
  role in SWD, 8–9, 24–28, 31*f*, 48, 49, 120, 138, 157
  who talk too much, 16–17, 143–144
teacher-student relationships, 118–119, 144, 145–146
team players, creating, 135–136
teamwork, 33–34, 135–136
technology, use of, 25–26
texts, choosing the, 22–24
textual evidence leader role, 106
three-question asker role, 95, 106
time, allotting for discussion, 24–28, 48
topic, choosing the first day, 22–24
topics, choosing the first day, 146
trust, 120

vocabulary leader role, 107

web grapher role, 106
workplace skills, 4, 10–11, 14, 33–34, 54–55
writing skills, 141

ABOUT THE AUTHOR

Alexis Wiggins is the founder and director of the Cohort of Educators for Essential Learning (CEEL), an organization that unites like-minded educators around the globe. She has worked as a high school and middle school English teacher in six different countries, and as an instructional coach for all subject areas. She has consulted with schools around the world on curriculum design, Spider Web Discussion, and the Harkness method. Wiggins helped the International Baccalaureate (IB) design their Approaches to Teaching and Learning for the diploma program initiative. She lives with her husband and two sons in The Woodlands, Texas, and teaches at the John Cooper School, where Wiggins also hosts Spider Web Discussion workshops and the CEEL Summer Symposium. You can find more information at www.ceelcenter.org, read her blog at www.ceelcenter.org/blog/, or follow Alexis on Twitter at @alexiswiggins.

Photo courtesy of Abdullah AlMahanna, on Instagram at amahanna.